Down on Court Five

Down on Court Five

Lessons Late in Life

VIVIAN WITKIND

Published by Royal Pom Publications

This is a work of non-fiction. However, to preserve
anonymity, some of the names of the people
portrayed in this book have been changed.

ISBN 13: 978-0-578-36817-7

First Edition Published 2022

This book is dedicated to my children.

PREFACE

When Jane Austen was my age, she'd been dead for 34 years. Thanks to extraordinary medical advances since the 18th century, age is likely to nibble away at you, bit by bit, sometimes annoyingly but often with pain. Lifespans have grown longer worldwide, especially for wealthy Western nations. Babies still die before they can focus their eyes and people of all ages have their lives cut too short for today's expectations. As I write this, more than 860,000 Americans have died from the Covid pandemic, no doubt nudging life expectancy downward. But I'm betting Jane Austen would have had time to write six more novels if she lived in the 21st century.

When you're young and healthy, frailty doesn't apply to you. All those old people, but not you. At the time of this story, Vincent, my eight-year-old grandson, still inhabited a self-affirming world where every birthday is a step up. It's a scary world for anyone who's been around for a while, however. Aging that applied to me first muscled its way into consciousness on my 21st birthday in February of 1967. That was nearly four years after Jack Kennedy was assassinated and exactly three years after the Beatles came to New York. I was about to graduate from college, and my generation of students was coming into its own, thinking for ourselves, rebelling and ready, or so we thought, to take over from the incorrigibly stupid older generation. We challenged an imperialist imperative that took on battling communism as far away as Vietnam. We challenged the inequality of the American social structure and economy in a gloriously consuming civil-rights movement. And, especially important for me at a women's college, we took a look at women's status and said, wait a minute, we deserve and demand equality with men, including reproductive rights that would help free us to become leaders as well as wives and mothers, presumably the kind of leaders who wouldn't support fruitless wars or systemic inequality of any kind.

To celebrate the U.S. age of majority, I flew from Boston to Palm Springs, California. My parents and grandparents each rented a house on the grounds of the spectacular La Quinta Resort a half hour down the road. The back nine of the golf course had not yet been constructed, and was open for horseback riding. The craggy, bare Santa Rosa Mountains looked down on a desert valley that would someday be relentlessly grassy. I took a long ride with a young group of teen and college-age kids, trotting and cantering when we could and playing games among the sand dunes. We only quit when the sun dipped below the mountains, which it does early there on a winter afternoon. In the evening, my grandfather, called Pop-pop, took us to a fine restaurant and ordered champagne. It arrived in such tall flutes I had to back away from the table to get the glass to my lips without spilling. The next morning, for the first time in my life, or the first time I noticed it, getting out of bed took a slow, careful effort. Anybody at any age will be the worse for immersion in activity that hasn't been practiced for a while. For me, that morning, waking up on the hard cot in the screen porch of my parents' vacation rental house, slowly dragging on shorts and trying to raise my arms enough to put on a top, I saw the shoulder-to-calf muscle pain as a harbinger of limits. I was going to grow old.

At 30, I had a husband, Jack, our first child, Josh, and was working on a doctorate in public policy at Ohio State University. I don't recall having time to think about the birthday, although I must have, because my generation of Sixties rebels told us not to trust anyone over 30, and there I was.

Our third child, Charlotte, was born when I was 40, eight years after Wit, our middle one. I saw it as a new lease on youth, ignoring the exhaustion.

The highlight of my career arrived when I was 50 in 1996. I was in the full power of middle age. It was in Cairo, where a group of U.S. consultants gave a week-long seminar on behalf of the Egyptian government to a couple of hundred people on the American way of public utility regulation. The professor who handled water utilities had the toughest job. There he was, lecturing on how water has a price, while from the room-length picture windows on our second-floor conference room we could all see the mighty Nile River, its full width and flowing with all the water anyone could need. I presented several segments on telecommunications. The internet was on its way, and the United States Congress had passed a law shattering the old organizational scheme. It was an unplowed field of incipient, life-changing technology. The folks in industry could hardly contain their commercial lust, and government had to figure out how to make sure the new playing field was both competitive for business and fulfilled the promise of barely imaginable gadgets and services at a fair price for customers, meaning everyone, everywhere.

At the time, presentations were printed on see-through individual PowerPoint slides. A group of silent Egyptian women changed the slides, one by one, on a machine that flashed them on a huge overhead screen. My group called the women 'the flippers'. One day towards the end of the week, I had a problem with my slides and went back to the room where the women worked to get it straightened out before my next presentation.

One of the younger women resorted the slides, looked at me meaningfully and said, "We are all so proud of you. You're up there with all the men and you talk as much as they do." I smiled and felt a surge of pride. That was the apogee of my work life.

By 2006, my parents, Char and Dick, had died. "You're not a grown-up until your parents go," Char had often told me. I thought that was ridiculous until it happened. Now, no one stood between Jack and me on the generational ladder. That was also the year I retired from my research job at Ohio State University. I remember lying on my bed, with my dog Scooby beside me in the afternoon, pursuing the luxury of a daytime nap. Jack had been diagnosed with progressive multiple sclerosis, but he was still able to walk and out and about that day. The house was quiet, way too quiet. *This is too good to be true*, I thought, *It won't last*. It was a bit like the twin towers in that immensely still morning blue sky a few years before when the world was about to come crashing down. An intensely narcissistic exaggeration, of course, but on a personal level, disaster could come in for a landing anytime, sending us tumbling into the darkness.

Aging eats at each of us differently, with the same ultimate outcome. Typically, what I'm getting used to seeing in my friends and older relatives is a slow decline followed by what the hospice folks call 'actively dying'. The medical wizards can fix all sorts of things that used to kill us fast. People walk around quite happily with hearts that can't hold their own pace, a fraught relationship with sugar or body parts gone missing.

My 70th birthday party was once again in La Quinta, at the house my brother and sister-in-law, Donnie and Lisal, were renting. Jack and I brought both our current Pomeranians, Scooby and young Russell. It was a spectacular do, with steak tartare to begin and coconut cake for a crowning finish. My younger sister Babette wrote a song especially for the occasion. Char had always written birthday songs, and I never imagined someone would create one for me. It was to the tune of "My Favorite Things" from *The Sound of Music*:

> *Writing her essays and playing her tennis,*
>
> *Keeping the doggies quite safe from all menace.*
>
> *Vacations with Jack and watching some tube,*
>
> *Vivian loves these, plus Russell and Scoob.*
>
> …
>
> *A woman who's in… her prime."*

The song was on target, including my fear for the dogs in La Quinta. Coyotes prowled the grounds at night, and one neighbor told me a coyote snatched her small dog in broad daylight on the golf course. The dog never made a sound: his neck was snapped instantly. But I damn well knew I wasn't in my prime. I remembered my grandmother at her 70th birthday party at home in Columbus, Ohio, and how the tears burst from her normal steady calm. Looking back, Hoo-hoo, as we numerous grandchildren called her, was most likely crying from surprise and gratitude at the over-the-top expression of love by my grandfather and her children. To my young eyes, the tears looked like regret as well. My grandmother had serious kidney disease. She was in decline and painfully aware of it, I thought, and might not make it to the next birthday. Her three daughters and son had given her an extraordinary gift, a badly needed, much larger building for central Ohio's Planned Parenthood, her most treasured cause. Hoo-hoo was a leader in the first wave of feminism, back at the beginning of the 20th century. Her four children announced the expanded space in a series of Char's songs, bawdy ones set to tunes from *My Fair Lady*. "We must write for the world to see, All the joys of the IUD" began a parody of "Loverly". "You can have your piece of arse and still have your peace of mind," belted out my aunts, uncle and mother. There, at my own 70th birthday party, I was conscious that something, maybe not renal failure, was going to get me, who knew how soon. Time's golf cart was rattling at my heels. Beyond the fairway lay eternal desert.

"The loneliest moment in someone's life is when they are watching their whole world fall apart, and all they can do is stare blankly."

F. Scott Fitzgerald

1

WAIT FOR IT

It was the last time the camera would catch my body intact. My breasts were being memorialized as I perched in a comfortable armchair at the long dinner table. On that late July evening in 2017, I was surrounded by my women's tennis team celebrating the end of the season at the New Albany Country Club on the outskirts of Columbus, Ohio. Buxom but unsmiling, I wore a tight white tank top. Presumably I was the only one about to lose a feature that is intimate, prominent and broadcasts womanhood.

I hadn't told my teammates about the lump.

A few weeks before, I wore a snug sports bra to a match and came home hot, sweaty and aware that the bra was rubbing something. As the welcome shower water sprayed down, I located the hard something at eight o'clock low on the left breast. My little brain whirred.

Just under the skin and sore to the touch, it was what they call 'a lump'.

"A lump," said the primary-care physician.

He sent me to the Spielman Breast Center for a diagnostic mammogram, more detailed than the usual screening. I walked slowly from the parking lot through automatic sliding doors, submitting myself to the process. Waited in line on the ground floor to introduce myself.

Waited. Registered. Wristband taped on. Elevator to imaging floor. Waited. Registered. Wristband checked. Waited. Time did not seem to be moving. I had an iPad, a copy of the *New York Times* in my lap and a hardcover book, *The Underground Railroad* by Colin Whitehead that my book group was reading that month. I didn't have the stomach right then for horrifyingly graphic images of slavery before the Civil War. Instead I riffled through my to-do list, which I kept in a four-by-six-inch notebook. One page per day for the A-list, folded over when the day is done. B-list, and a C-Z list were at the back of the book. The C-Z list lumped together tasks that might never get done. I wondered if that was about to expand exponentially.

An aide handed me a robe and led me to a bin to store my clothes. The gown was surprisingly thick and warm. A nurse escorted me down a corridor of starkly bright fluorescent lights to yet another waiting area, my identifying wristband on one arm and the locker key dangling from a band on the other. It was a Wednesday, so the *Times* crossword puzzle was easy. I finished it. Waited. Despite the robe, I felt not only cold but naked.

"Come on in," said a different nurse and checked my wristband to make sure I was who she was expecting.

Cold, hard metal squeezed my breasts into flapjacks in multiple directions for multiple images, not the usual couple of clicks. Another room, with a bed with a soft mattress. I sat tensely, rather than lying down, once again waiting, this time for the radiologist. She was a young doctor, a slim woman with long blonde hair in a neat ponytail. My hearing aids told her I was deaf, and she perched comfortingly on the bed so I would be sure to hear her.

The lump was "of concern," she said in a soft, kind voice, but assured me the vast majority were benign. "It's about the size of a peanut." This turned out to be a standard way of explaining lumps. Smaller than a peanut is good; bigger, bad. She scheduled a biopsy.

Shelled or unshelled, I wondered. *Two fruits or one? Hazelnut size, good. Brazil nut, bad.*

A frisson of fear descended. My hands and feet felt like blocks of ice. I took the doctor's supportive compassion as a bad sign. The odds were that the news was something way too real.

Back in my car, I gripped the steering wheel and paused to catch my breath, looking out at the crowded parking lot, seeing nothing. I was a tangle of emotions: sad, scared and shaky. I had to keep it together but needed a distraction, some instant comfort. Extra sugar was ordinarily verboten, but this was an emergency. Eat dessert first; life is uncertain, I reminded myself. On my way home, I pulled into Whit's Frozen Custard, a local joint, and sat on a patio bench to consume a scoop of chocolate on a cake cone as slowly as possible in the hot July sun. I was alone on a hard stool, my tongue seeking out the spots that were about to turn to liquid and taming them before they dripped. At that moment it was the best ice cream, frozen custard, frozen yogurt or sherbet I ever tasted. I savored the last bites of crisp cone and melting sweet-sour custard. I headed home, deciding not to make a big deal with Jack until I knew for certain. I couldn't be sick. I was my disabled husband's caregiver. Joan Didion would call that magical thinking.

A couple of days later deep in a long afternoon, the phone buzzed angrily. I was at my desk in my loft office, typing in some checks to be printed. I'd taken over the financial tasks from Jack a year or so before when it turned out he hadn't paid the water bill and the township was about to cut us off. His fingers wouldn't work the keyboard anymore, and he'd been too proud to tell me.

"Your biopsy came back," was the first thing the kind doctor said on the phone. "I'm sorry to say that it shows a type of cancer."

"What type?" Not that I was going to understand her answer.

"Invasive ductile carcinoma. I'll be fixing you up with a doctor to take over from here."

"Great," I said, feeling numb and stunned.

After hanging up, I concentrated on maintaining calm, listening to the purring coo of mourning doves in the trees outside my window. I looked around my cozy loft nest overlooking the first floor. Bookcases and filing cabinets. A comfortable couch upholstered in cherry-red. A narrow staircase that led down to the family room, our mutual, special nest. Above the couch and beyond the windows a glimmer of the hybrid American elm Jack and I planted 20 years ago had reached some 40 feet of leafy, green splendor. True

American elms died out over a century ago. The Columbus-born humorist James Thurber had an aunt who died of the same disease that was killing the elms, or so he said. I turned to look past the computer screen to a framed black-and-white photo of my uncle in an Air Force uniform, and my father in his Navy lieutenant one, two tall young men, handsome and pensive, in the early days of World War II, long gone now, both felled by cancer.

Sorrow belted me in the gut. A malignant lump. And invasive, yet. An army with a beachhead ready to advance inland.

I sat motionless at my desk for several minutes, trying to think through what was happening and what hell lay ahead. There would be more waiting rooms. My world of comfortable routines was coming to a screeching halt, replaced by tectonic change I could not yet imagine.

My office connected to our bedroom through the long, two-sink corridor of the bathroom. I could hear Jack and Steve Buck, our home health aide, laughing at one of their mutual in-jokes as Steve dressed him after a nap.

I walked through the bathroom. Steve had my husband outfitted in a bright checked shirt with a button-down collar. He was just slipping a pair of brown loafers on Jack's feet, the last step.

"Problem," I told Jack, looking down at his upturned, smiling face. In his state-of-the-art electric wheelchair, he still looked like a man in charge. Seven years earlier, in June 2010, he'd had his own gruesome bout of nose cancer, which left him with no sense of smell and an indentation between his eyes that marked the spot where the surgeon had to go up almost to the brain to chase a malignant tail. I called it Jack's 'on/off' button.

It was MS that crippled him further day by day. By 2017 Jack couldn't roll over in bed. Most of his fingers were curled stiffly, though he could still wield a fork and get the food to his mouth. Falls were of the personal kind, in the middle of a transfer to or from the bathroom, wheelchair and bed. I'd call the emergency squad, and strong men would get him up. We feared diseases and conditions that wouldn't kill most people, but could zap him in his vulnerable state. The dangers were pneumonia, urinary-tract infections and humiliating bedsores. It was before the novel coronavirus hit.

How would Jack react to my admission that I had cancer? It's a terrifying word. When people hear it, they immediately think of 'death'. Wondering how to tell him without using the dreaded C-word, I simply blurted out, "I might be in trouble."

"It'll be fine," he replied quietly. He was seemingly unworried, as I struggled to hide my low-grade panic.

It was a relief that he wasn't taking this as seriously as I, or was trying to appear not to. With luck, it would indeed be okay, and I wouldn't be letting him down.

I wanted Jack's comfort, but knew he didn't have the strength to worry about me. The primary purpose of his every minute was to stay alive himself. MS slowly robs you of the ability to move. He was diagnosed in 1993, when he was 46, and the disease had spun a cruel, strangling web through his life. He fought every incremental loss.

That night, after I told Jack I might be in trouble, I went through the routine of getting him into bed, doling out his six pills and watching him shakily bring the water glass to his mouth. I tucked a towel under his chin, so if he spilled it I wouldn't have to change his T-shirt. While he drank I lifted our two current fluffy Pomeranians, fox-faced Aristotle and perpetually bewildered-looking Bertrand Russell, onto the bed. We were a party of four.

Jack passed me the glass and reached for my hand. "I'm sorry, Vivian," he said, looking wistful, "I'm useless."

Early in the spring of 1993, Jack had casually asked me, "Have you noticed I'm walking funny? I'm wobbling." I hadn't paid attention. A few months later, in August, when we were on our way from Florida to Columbus in the minivan, we stopped in a North Carolina town with craft and antique shops, an attraction for me, though not for him. From behind Jack I could see the wobbling. He looked like he was drunk and pretending not to be.

In Columbus, he saw a neurologist, who waved away the problem as though it would miraculously vanish. That didn't stop the wobbling. We appealed to a doctor friend, a rheumatologist, who made a house call.

"It has to be a central nervous system disease," said the doctor, sitting on our living room couch. "The hair loss on your legs is the clue." He couldn't help looking a bit pleased to be able to make a diagnosis.

After our friend left, I wondered where Jack had gone. Without a word, he had slunk out to the pond beyond our sloping lawn and was standing there, in the twilight, facing the dark, algae-ridden water at the shallow end.

Slipping up beside him at the water's edge, I clasped his hand tightly. The night sky darkened above us. As we stood in silence, I could see the stars coming out and the silver-faced moon seemed closer. I didn't have anything to comfort him with but my presence.

There are two basic kinds of MS. The first is relapsing-remitting, which means you have an attack of the disease, then it relents and you regain at least some of your former abilities. The second is progressive. It is relentless. That's the kind Jack turned out to have. He fought it every inch of the way.

The ability to walk was the first thing he began to lose. Eventually, Jack admitted canes into his wardrobe, several of them, all formed from shiny, mottled hardwood. One had a bone handle; another, a carving of what looked like a crouching black panther. They were the kind of canes you imagine old-fashioned London barristers carrying. Not for Jack the sturdy, modern, metal cane with three-pronged feet that bespeaks fragility rather than a gentlemanly limp.

Then there was the evening he came home from an office event and showed me a shattered cell-phone screen.

"What happened?" I'd asked.

"I fell."

"What do you mean… was it in the breast pocket of your jacket and you fell straight down flat on your chest so it broke like that?"

He had to admit it, covering up with one of his happy-go-lucky grins. I knew how much he hated having to be picked up from the floor.

From a cane, Jack went directly to a sitting position because he thought a walker made you look older and sicker. We bought a red, fold-up, three-wheel scooter plus a fold-up manual wheelchair with bicycle wheels that could be popped on and off. The tires were light as they could be, but not suited for rough terrain. Either one would fit in the trunk of his aubergine Mercedes. Our family tradition was to own fire-engine red cars, and he'd tried to get away with deep purple by calling it dark red. We added hand controls for the car. He could still go downtown to his work in commercial real estate.

The electric scooter was perfect for handicapped seats at Ohio State football games. The ushers and Jack got to know each other by name. Within a few years, Jack and I both retired from our day jobs and went farther afield, a lot farther afield. If we couldn't take the heavy scooter, I was the pusher of the manual wheelchair.

The next thing to go was driving. Jack had always been a superb driver, and I was perfectly happy being the passenger. First we replaced our lovely purple Mercedes with a scarlet Toyota Sienna minivan. It had a ramp, and he could slot his electric wheelchair into the driver's place. The steering controls were on the wheel. Later, we had the van altered so I had the driver's seat and he could insert the wheelchair to my right. Eventually, when Jack could not stand by himself, and I certainly couldn't haul him out of bed, we bought a stand-and-lift machine that pulled him upright and allowed us to roll him to the wheelchair and set him slowly down.

I still loved to look into Jack's blue eyes, the sparkling, light blue of the Caribbean close to the shore, reproduced in both our daughters. He wore coke-bottle glasses, so I was privileged to be almost the only one who ever saw those calming sea-blue eyes without a thick glass shield. I could still detect a glint of the youthful desire and intensity that brought us together. Through 44 years of marriage we were companions, neither one trying to outshine the other. He knew my flaws: vain, competitive, poor at financial calculations. I knew his: prone to avoid facing problems straight on and, back when he was able-bodied, an aversion to manual tasks.

I squeezed his hand and smiled with my eyes. "Your job is to keep going."

If Jack had not been crippled emotionally as well as physically by his own disease, he would have been on Google and talking with our doctor daughter, Wit. He would have wanted to find the best breast-cancer treatment in the country, or the world, and persuade me to fly post-haste to the Mayo Clinic or MD Anderson Cancer

Center. As far as I could tell, the Ohio State medical megalopolis in Columbus was fine for what I had. I wasn't going to run around the country for something better.

Cancer terrified Jack. He was only in his early twenties when his mother died. So young and already so deeply wounded. We talked about it early in our dating, which must have been sometime in 1971. I can't recall the conversation precisely, but think it was at a restaurant after a movie and went something like this:

"Have you heard of Elisabeth Kübler-Ross?" he'd asked out of the blue as I'm betting we consumed fluffy, syrup-soaked piles of the house specialty at the International House of Pancakes, one of our go-to places. Kübler-Ross's path-breaking book *On Death and Dying* came out in 1969.

"No," I answered, wondering why he was bringing it up.

"She wrote about the stages of grief." A tiny pause and he said, "My mother died."

"When? And of what?"

"Last year."

I waited, possibly while cleaning up a bit of sweet-smelling maple syrup with the next piece of my favorite blueberry pancakes.

"Breast cancer," he said after a pause with downcast eyes. "And she never ever talked about it. I was living at home, going to Franklin, so I saw it all and couldn't say anything." His home was around the corner from my parents in the suburban enclave of Bexley. Franklin College, now Franklin University, is in downtown Columbus.

"She went to a hospital out in the sticks when she was dying, so nobody would know." It endeared me to my date to hear how he, as a scared young man, had to watch his mother decline, never using the horrific C-word.

When I was absorbing my own diagnosis, that summer of 2017, Ohio State was running an ad campaign with huge billboards proclaiming 'there is no routine [fill in the body part] cancer'. For the customer that's the bitter truth. From the point of view of medical practice, it's a flaming lie, thank God. Layer upon layer of routine had been skillfully built up to create a treatment sequence based on accurate diagnoses, solid statistics, lab-tested medications and skilled, trained practitioners. The patient goes from waiting room to waiting room according to a plan, taking the elevator up or down, turning left or right because someone knows the drill. Fourth floor or second floor? Surgery or chemo? Or the building next door that does radiology? If the choices get complicated and the doctors start talking about treatment before they're sure of the diagnosis, which happens more often than we want to know, then it's second opinion time, not before that.

We'd always slept in an ordinary king-size bed, but when Jack started to need propping up, we bought one split into two twins, each with its own controls to position feet and head Goldilocks perfect. You could choose how soft or hard you wanted the mattress. There was a button to wake your partner if they snored, which Jack seemed to think valuable. We used a king-sized top sheet and blanket, so theoretically we could still cuddle. But it was difficult.

That night, I moved a sleepy Pomeranian, tilted to my side and reached across the crack to Jack's cool, soft arm as he lay on his back, unable to roll towards me. I struggled clumsily across the crack and lay against him along his right side and stroked his soft cotton T-shirt. He did his best to maneuver his arm around me. I could tell it was uncomfortable. I only had about six inches of width to balance in. I moved back to my side.

After a blisteringly bad day, I was ready to call it a night, but my mind raced into the existential wilds.

This is bad. This is shitty. Shitfuck. I'm not supposed to get sick. Fuckshit. It's Jack who's sick. It's not my turn. What time will Steve be in? I need more helpers. Where do I get those? Need a diversion. Three two-syllable words. Prancing chestnut ponies. Ordinary people. Okay, six syllables, either two or three words. Ductal carcinoma. This is not working. Please, God. You don't believe in God, stupid. Try poetry. 'Some vengeful god from up the sky.' Not that one. 'Up above a high Ohio, like a dime on a piano.'

The night stretched long and uneasy.

Willy nilly, the cancer diagnosis opened up buried memories. My father died in 2003 without ever talking to me about the spreading malignancy, just like Jack's mother never talked to him. And I didn't raise it with my dad. I knew he had had prostate cancer some ten years before that, and was vaguely aware that something else went wrong. But my mother was the sick one, with COPD (chronic obstructive pulmonary disease). She had to drag around an oxygen tank for two years. A full-time nursing staff cared for my mother at home. After she succumbed that May, a nurse came to me and said, "We didn't know your dad was sick. He never said a word."

An old family friend, a general surgeon by trade, visited from New York and stopped me in my parents' driveway to talk. "I thought I was here to see a friend," he'd said, looking bewildered. "I didn't know he was terminal." I didn't know what terminal looked like, but realized it had to be obvious.

Hiding, like my father and Jack's mother, is an old-fashioned way of handling the disease, back when it was shameful and not spoken of. Spilling the news would be hard, but there was no getting around it.

I phoned our two daughters, Wit, an emergency-room physician in Phoenix, and Charlotte, an advertising copywriter in New York. The former was right on the case, of course, and immediately asked, "What kind of cancer?"

"Invasive ductal carcinoma. The tumor is the size of a peanut."

"Do you know the plan yet? Surgery, then maybe chemo or radiation, or both?"

"Not yet."

Wit was as calm as if she was taking a patient history. That helped. Charlotte had enough experience with her father's illnesses that she readily knew the right questions: "What are the next steps? Who is your doctor?" She has a delicate soul but is as professional as Wit and handled the news well, at least while we were on the phone.

I headed west from our suburban house through downtown Columbus to pick up Vincent, our four-year-old grandson, for our weekly get-together at his home in Upper Arlington. It was one of those pristine, older suburbs that people choose for the school system and could use more diversity. Josh, my son, and his wife Lorraine moved there soon after they married. Upper Arlington has leafy parks, old-growth trees and broad sidewalks, many wide enough for two strollers to pass each other.

That day, when I needed to give Josh my bad news, I planned to strap Vincent into his toddler car seat and take him to lunch at the Chef-o-Nette, a cheap greasy spoon across the way from the Northam Park tennis courts. Vincent could order mac 'n' cheese, his favorite lunch, with the promise that if he ate enough I would give him a quarter for a gumball for dessert from the bubble-shaped machine at the check-out counter. We would follow up with a trip to the library. When I arrived at their home, there was no sign of Vincent, but a cardboard box took up half the living-room floor in the midst of scattered Legos and a colorful blaze of shiny metal Hot Wheels. Sammy slunk into the room to greet me, weaving around my legs and swishing his stripy tail. He was a friendly, long orange fellow who adored my grandson. I rarely thought of cats as companionable, but Sammy was as loving as any dog.

As I bent down to stroke Sammy, I said loudly to Josh. "I wonder where Vincent is?"

The box wiggled. "Surprise!" shouted Vincent in his falsetto voice as he popped out through the flap and fell into my arms. He hugged me ferociously, knocking my purse off my shoulder. He smelled clean and fresh, young and healthy. My only grandchild seemed to have grown a half inch since I saw him the week before. I remembered him lying on my stomach to nap when he was a baby and smelling his sweet head and stroking his wispy hair, then blonde. Where would I be when he was a stinky, sweaty teenager? If I were still around, he'd tower over me and he'd better be careful not to knock me over.

"There's news," I told my son as we stood in his living room. "I have C A N C E R. There will be S U R G E R Y."

Josh's eyes narrowed at my spelled-out announcement. From a long, spindly baby he had somehow become a stout middle-aged man with thinning, silvering hair. How I could have a child in his mid-forties, I did not know.

Vincent would have asked many questions I did not want to answer. He was alarmingly precocious, and his parents were scrupulously frank with him. When he was about two, I taught him a song from Pogo, the possum, from olden-day comics: *Twiggle, twiggle lily starch Whaddy rumble whaddy arch…*

Later, Lorraine, a mother who likes things correct, heard Vincent singing it one night, no doubt quite sweetly, in his bedroom. "What on earth?" she asked. Josh, who I raised with an appreciation for nonsense, knew exactly what his son was warbling. The silly parents corrected him and taught him the regular, twinkly words.

Only a few months before this visit, when Vincent asked about dying, his parents explained the inevitability of mortality. A bit later, when we were out having dinner, he told a skinny young waitress, while tucking into his creamy mac 'n' cheese, "You're gonna die." She smiled and said, "Let's not push it."

"We'll talk later," I told Josh while Vincent got his shoes on to venture forth with me. I knew Lorraine and Josh would help however they could. This would ordinarily make me feel guilty, but it was C A N C E R.

The next day, with as much "oh, by the way" as I could pull off, I called Bobby, Donnie and Babette, my three siblings, then Mary, my 88-year-old aunt who had only recently given up her steady game of tennis. I called my closest friends, allowing the news to escape my tight throat, and taking in the immediate sympathy as an infusion of sunlight. Turning cancer into words made it both truer and momentarily more painful. If you don't talk to people, however, the secret becomes a tumor. I did not share the news with anybody on the tennis team. A whole gaggle commiserating at the end of the season would be too much attention. It was still high summer. We were still playing.

My usually predictable summer life was knocked to smithereens, not to mention my usually predictable autumn life, not to mention the rest of my life, for which I had plans. Like staying alive. Stage-one breast cancer is quite treatable these days. It was reasonable to bet on stage one. I knew women who had bouts of breast cancer decades ago and were still going strong. So far there was every prospect that the cancer hadn't broken out of its semi-permeable cage. It would probably not kill me, at least in round one. The medical system would dictate the near future, but maybe leave me alone for a while afterwards, a golden period of time when I could ignore that vexing issue of mortality.

It could not be ignored. Cancer invades both body and mind.

2

GRAVITY ONE, ENTROPY ZERO, 2010

"He's likely to look as much dead as alive," I warned Charlotte as I lifted the intercom phone to request permission to enter the intensive-care unit. "It may be hard to recognize him." I was unnervingly right. I flinched as we walked in. It didn't help that the view of Jack was straight on, since the hospital bed was tilted to an easy-chair position. Over his nose a contraption like a World War I gas mask connected to a noisily motoring oxygen source by a six-inch-wide accordion tube. The upper half of his face was swollen. My post-surgical husband rocked his head up and down arrhythmically, slowly thrashing like a prehistoric fish dredged from the sea, or an alien dragged from his home planet to inhospitable earth. His hair was clotted thick with the tang of sour-smelling dried blood, and a broad, bloody bandage spread across his forehead. He pulled his head up off the mattress and let it down again after a few seconds, then immediately with great effort pulled it back up. His hands were in restraints tied to the bed like a mental patient. Tubes pierced the inner side of his right elbow. The left arm scrabbled to get to his face and could almost do it. The wrist strap was too long. Our daughter grabbed his hand to keep it in check.

"What is it?" I asked him. "Your head?"

He shook it. He couldn't talk because of the oxygen mask.

I thought he might be in pain from the tubes rubbing him at the hospital gown's neck, which was stained pink. "Here?"

Ragged head shake.

I looked closely at the band that held on the oxygen mask. It was so tight that the flesh bulged out on either side. I went into the hall and summoned the ICU nurse, who came and loosened the mask. She called a doctor to see if it could be removed yet.

Charlotte asked if that was better.

Jack nodded.

A team came to dial down the oxygen, and we stood outside. Seeing him in that desperate state, so battered and bloodied, was breaking my heart. I was shivering in the warm room.

"Thank you for warning me," said Charlotte, who was shaken herself. I was glad I had warned both of us. From the corridor, I heard a loud groan and felt enormous relief at the throaty but inimitable sound.

He's back, I thought, relieved.

The doctors at Presbyterian Hospital, nicknamed Presby, part of the University of Pittsburgh Medical Center, had assured us an hour earlier, that July day in 2010, that the operation to remove the cancer deep up Jack's nose was successful, and the only reason he was in intensive care was that it took longer than expected, resulting in a short-term need for extra oxygen. The major work had been done endoscopically through the nasal cavity. He would be out of the hospital in a couple of days.

Just because someone sounds like himself doesn't mean he's all there, however. Jack certainly wasn't back. He was a weak and muddled warrior, and it was a full week before we got him safely home.

A non-medical observer can get an idea of how sick a post-op patient is by the number of things attached to him. Back in the ICU, now that Jack was calm, I counted the bodily intrusions, protective coverings and vital-sign monitors that would have to be removed before I could get him back. Eighteen.

"We have your phone number," the nurse said cheerfully as Charlotte and I were about leave for the night at around 7:30 p.m.

I felt like a slacker. Was I supposed to sleep in the ICU waiting room like some other people I saw there? Definitely not. I had no indication that things were off track. The hospital staff could jolly well reach me, and if Jack took a turn for the worse, I could race back to the hospital within 15 minutes.

I took half a sleeping pill. Charlotte wanted one, too, and though it was prescription medicine I gave her the other half. I turned up the air conditioning. The room at the Hampton Inn, airless and stifling, felt like a sauna. I assured myself that the best surgeons with the best equipment had gone in to dig out the invasive mass of out-of-control cells on their way to overwhelming the orderly processes of my husband's body. The doctors believed they did their job well and fully. The patient looked like someone who underwent surgery inside his skull, no less and no more.

The first time I noticed something was wrong was the previous winter in January 2010, when we were on a cruise to South America and Antarctica. We had daily laundry service and every day most of Jack's handkerchiefs went in the laundry bag. My dapper dude was reduced to using Kleenex.

"Why are you going through so many handkerchiefs?" I'd asked him.

"My right nostril keeps dripping," he'd said.

It was a clear, steady leak of fluid. Even then this seemed odd. Maybe it had something to do with the bitingly cold, dry air of the Antarctic Peninsula, I reasoned. Once we got back home, I persuaded him to call our internist, who put him on allergy meds, a reassuring solution. A couple of weeks later the nostril started to bleed slightly.

"Should I call the doctor?" Jack asked. It was April by then.

"Absolutely," I said, "call her."

He did not. Should I have picked up the phone? Should I have smelled danger earlier? I was not paying attention.

Three days later at lunch by himself at the Clarmont, a popular landmark restaurant for business lunches, Jack's nose hemorrhaged and bled all over the white table linen, dying it bright red. The staff wanted to call 911, but he insisted on driving himself, leaving me a message that he was coming home. Instead, with a little more rationality he drove, gushing blood all the way, to the Mount Carmel East emergency room. Our son Josh was there with him before I was. The offending organ had a strip of gauze over it to soak up the ooze and the right nostril was packed with more stuff. Jack's expensive sky-blue knit shirt and khaki slacks were splattered in blood like the first flicks of a nascent abstract painting. The emergency-room physician thought there was a polyp up the nose.

Jack was rattled and worried. I knew what he was thinking and teased him. "You've decided you have terminal brain cancer."

Surgery to remove the polyp was scheduled quickly and taken care of in May. We were both happy to see the end of it. Even when the ENT surgeon called to say the biopsy from the operation had come back and he was referring Jack to a specialist, I was oblivious.

"He said it was benign," Jack reported back to me. I've wondered since what the ENT surgeon really said.

Only a month later, when we saw Dr. Bradley Otto at the Ohio State University hospital on June 17th, did I have an inkling of the seriousness of the situation. I expected him to say Jack had something that needed to be watched in case it ever turned nasty. Dr. Otto, a personable, lean young doc with warm brown eyes, asked Jack what he had been told.

"They said it's a polyp," Jack said. "What's the difference between a polyp and a tumor?"

"A polyp is one kind of tumor," the doctor explained cheerfully, "And the biopsy showed an olfactory neuroblastoma, which is 'a cancer'."

Uh oh, I thought. *This guy is laying that word on Jack, the disease he's most terrified of. He shouldn't tell him it's a cancer.*

My mind made a knight's move, and I thought, *he has cancer. The doc is telling us my husband has cancer.* It's not just 'a' cancer. The way people usually say it is 'cancer'. Understanding came to me like cold skewers thrust up my nose. The doctor forged ahead on different approaches to the operation Jack must have and what tests were needed before that could be resolved. He wanted an MRI and a CT scan, referrals to radiation oncology, neurosurgery, and maybe ophthalmology and hematology.

Dr. Otto had just come on board at OSU after a residency at Pittsburgh in endoscopic cancer surgery. There was a new surgical procedure for Jack's trouble that was less invasive than the traditional approach but took a neurosurgeon as well as a head-and-neck guy. The neurosurgeon on Dr. Otto's team would not be on board for a couple of months. He spelled olfactory neuroblastoma for me and recommended we look at the American Cancer Society and James Cancer Hospital websites.

Jack looked calm, crossed one leg over the other casually and smiled as if hearing a lunchtime story at the Clarmont from a friend. The words barreled at me: 'oncology', 'radiology', 'the James'. It was too fast, like someone slamming balls by me at the tennis net. The doctor, it struck me, was way too happy. I reckoned that nose cancer was his job, and a patient had arrived whom he could help. I learned later that his first-born son had arrived the day before. He was suffused with joy that couldn't be hidden.

The day of surgery on Jack's nose to remove the nasty aesthesioneuroblastoma (another word for the foreign nose object, and even harder to spell) began with a hotel wake-up call at 4 a.m. The three of us headed for the hospital, where time moved as slowly as an IV drip, Charlotte and I doing our best to be supportively normal and Jack contemplating his hospital wristband. At the hotel he had taken Ativan with his last permitted sip of water to abate the anxiety, but it wasn't doing the whole job.

Finally, just before 9 a.m., the time for separation came. Charlotte and I headed for the 11th-floor cafeteria for coffee, doughnuts and blueberry yogurt, before settling down on the second floor for the long wait. My daughter and I are both barely five-feet tall. In this case it was an advantage. We figured out how to make napping space out of four armchairs, two for each. An electronic message board gave the status of the patients, rather like airport arrivals and departures. Ours was 'in surgery', exactly where he was supposed to be for at least the next six hours.

Left to ourselves, Charlotte and I often gravitated towards arguments on the order of college bull sessions. The kind of talk that took place at two in the morning when both parties are supposed to be writing the paper due the day after tomorrow. It was a way to alleviate boredom and amuse ourselves, like a fencing match. I had to be careful not to take the rubber off the rapier tip, however. Charlotte was 24 in 2010, but I still had the power to wound her.

Our busy youngest child was extremely thoughtful and caring to come to Pittsburgh. Charlotte was in graduate school studying fashion at the Parsons School of Design in New York. As a student on a tight budget, her outfits were nonetheless brilliantly coordinated thrift-store finds. Unlike me, she always had style. In Florida, when Charlotte was four, we shopped for new sandals at a beachy boutique. She picked out some bright gold ones. I was surprised and looked at the salesperson as if to say, "What the heck?"

"Some of us are gold-lamé sandals," she said, "And some of us are…" A pause while she eyed me up and down, "Talbots." I do tend to wear middle-of-the-road, middle-aged straight-out-of-a-catalogue clothing.

Nibbling more of the waiting area's free graham crackers in between sips of burnt coffee, I was starting to feel sick, and my mouth tasted like fish that died on a tarry beach. I needed to spar. I had brought along *Let the Great World Spin* to read.

Charlotte flicked through it and formed an opinion. "There are all these endless lists," she complained, showing me the introduction. "You can't just do lists."

"He's showing the infinite variety of New York," I said. "Life in all its crazy complexity that somehow works."

"What's it about?"

"I believe it's tied together by the tightrope walker. The one who walked between the World Trade Center towers in the Eighties."

A woman across from us was working on a laptop, but I was sure she was listening.

"I wish everyone didn't look at me and think I'm 13 years old," said Charlotte, my dainty, sparkly-eyed daughter.

The woman's lips creased into a slight smile without looking up from her laptop.

"Look at it this way," I told Charlotte. "How many adults can sleep on a couple of small waiting-room armchairs pushed together?"

A large family across from us had a visit from a doctor, who explained in a gentle bedside voice that they did not know much yet but had operated as soon as the patient, apparently the paternal head of the family, arrived unconscious with a deep concussion. "The situation is dire," the doctor told them unceremoniously. My eyes were closed, and I knew I shouldn't be listening to their hardship but was enthralled by the word 'dire'. You see it in print, but rarely hear it out loud.

At around lunchtime, Charlotte went to the cafeteria, while I waited in case a doctor showed up with news. She came back with sushi, pizza and tapioca pudding. A bit past 5 p.m., or more than eight hours after the operation had started, a receptionist told us the job was done and we could talk to the doctors upstairs on the third floor. A staff member led us up in the slow, oppressive box of an elevator.

Upstairs, Dr. Paul Gardner, the neurosurgeon, bespectacled and with sandy hair, so handsome he looked like a movie-star version of a doctor on *Grey's Anatomy* or *ER*, came to meet us, along with Dr. Carl Snyderman, the ENT surgeon, Dr. Otto's equivalent.

"It took longer than we expected because we had to chase a tail of the tumor up towards the brain," he said, and explained that they had to drill a small hole between the eyes to get to the nasty tail but filled the hole with mesh and covered it with forehead skin so it would be almost unnoticeable. It was, in fact, an obvious dimple. That was what became the 'on/off' button.

When Dr. Gardner was done explaining, I peppered him and the surgeon beside him with questions. "Had the cancer reached beyond the dura to the brain itself?"

"No. We did an MRI and it looks like we got it. No involvement as far as we can tell."

"Were you able to establish margins consistent with oncological principles?" I asked Dr. Carl Snyderman, tall, middle-aged and distinguished, with the stance of an athlete. My way of coping with Jack's diagnosis had been to read as much as possible. I felt like a parrot but got the sentence out. The answer was "yes, adequate margins."

Before leaving, Dr. Snyderman gave me a comforting hug around the shoulders. As uptight as they make them, he was probably thinking.

"Geez," Charlotte said. "All I wanted to ask was when we could see him, but with your questions that sounded stupid. And I have a crush on Dr. Gardner."

"You take Dr. Gardner and I'll take Dr. Snyderman." It was hard not to love the people who were saving your loved one's life.

Back in the reception area, I asked Charlotte's obvious, sensible question. We could see him anytime, but would have to phone into the ICU before being permitted entry. We opted to head back to the motel and freshen up.

Following that very first visit with Dr. Otto at OSU, waiting for more tests and to schedule surgery, Jack didn't want to tell anybody about his new illness. I felt at risk of levitating or spinning into fragments. As a kid, I read Buck Rogers, a comic strip with a logo of the hero spaceman's head against a field of stars. It scared me. He had no helmet, and I knew you couldn't breathe in outer space.

To lighten the evenings while we waited for the next steps, we watched the funniest movies we could find.

"Why did you rent *Roxanne*?" I asked. "It's about a nose."

Jack had forgotten the *Cyrano* angle and only remembered Steve Martin and romance.

To stay in touch with the ground, I took the dogs for long walks, seeking out woodland paths and suburban sidewalks I'd never tried before and feeding Scooby, the old guy, a baby aspirin in between because, though still eager to go as far as I wanted, he had arthritis.

Tears came to my eyes at odd times. My beloved had been socked in the head. Yet he was already suffering from one terrible disease. It was infuriating that he could be hit by another. At the time, the MS diagnosis was already 15 years before and he had been stable for close to a decade. I had gotten used to it as something you live with. Cancer you die from. I imagined Jack's bespoke sports jackets and fancy loafers with tassels and kilties sitting unworn in the closet. I wondered if his T-shirts would still smell like him and whether I would wear them to sleep in. I imagined going alone to parties or to dinner with other widows.

We had to endure Father's Day and Josh's 35th birthday party over the weekend without letting on a thing even to family. I wondered whether Jack felt that if he said nothing about the cancer, it wasn't there. But it wasn't my place to question his choice. Here was a guy who on business issues never gave up, yet he was detached. Here was a guy who had taken charge of his MS treatment and fought it daily, yet he seemed passive.

I remembered seeing a snake with a half-devoured frog under some bushes when I was little and calling to my uncle to save the frog. The back half was already inside the snake. It looked out vacantly under the sharp eyes of its killer. Because I was howling, my uncle used a stick to successfully pry out the frog, which sat and waited for the snake to start up again. It was alive but as good as dead because it had given up.

I had to figure this out. Decisions as pressing as they get bore down on us. What treatment and where could be life-or-death choices. And I had to define my own job. That was to take care of Jack, shore him up. To do that, I needed information, which required detective work. It would thrust me down a rabbit hole of reading and researching geography and interdependencies I've never wanted or tried to map or navigate: the mysterious realm of the human body, where most of the time every cell knows its job and contributes to an organ and a system that works so well the happy human being has no idea what is going on, like a tightrope walker far above the bustle and smells and noise of bicycle-delivery kids, diesel-fume-spewing buses, cell-phone texters, pizza parlors, bed-bug exterminators, garbage scows, clicking high heels, cathedrals, shop windows, rasping iron gates, street vendors selling roasting chestnuts, marble statues, baby carriages and poodles. Somehow I needed to know enough to ask the right questions, the ones that would prompt guidance.

I was looking for information on a rare cancer, which helped my internet search. Not many articles had been published on tumors of the nasal cavity. When I began digging deeper, Dr. Snyderman's name came up. I printed, underlined and starred whole sections of the ENT surgeon's article on 'Principles of Endonasal Oncological Surgery', pressing hard with a smudging blue roller ball. I felt less helpless, and therefore less hopeless. This was a treatable disease with a five-year survival rate of close to 80 percent using an endoscopic approach.

The MRI ordered by Dr. Otto showed a tiny white spot on Jack's brain. He wondered if that should be investigated further. We met with Dr. A, a neurosurgeon at Ohio State, in a tiny room with an examination bed of shiny bile-green vinyl. Something mounted on the wall had been removed and three blue studs and pimpled nail holes remained in the discolored paint. The surgeon declared with no possibility of disagreement that Jack needed a brain biopsy to see if the lesion in the posterior of the temporal lobe was cancer or not. He would be glad to operate. The surgery would last ten hours and the patient would be in the hospital for a couple of weeks. I didn't mention to Jack that the method the good doctor was proposing had a morbidity rate of close to a third and a slew of nasty post-operative side effects.

I asked about the invasiveness of a biopsy, and he gave me a lecture on how all surgery is invasive. It's an advertising ploy, he allowed, to talk about 'non-invasive' or 'minimally invasive' surgery. The most important issue is the goal, he said, without specifying what that was.

The doctor was dark, lean and slick-looking. Italian or maybe South American. As he relaxed against the door with ankles crossed I could imagine a cigarette hanging from his lips while he lounged by the Spanish Steps with some pals, admiring the tight-skirted, big-breasted signorinas as they strolled by. *Oily*, I thought, while remembering I must not judge a surgeon by his looks or personality. They had to be decisive or they would not have the courage to wield their scalpels. I thought of a pop song of my youth, *I was a Teenage Brain Surgeon*.

"I can do it tomorrow or Wednesday," he said decisively, "I go to Europe Thursday."

Shocked that a doctor could be so cavalier, I swallowed hard and said we would get back to him.

The next stop was a PET scan in Doan Hall. Time is distorted when you spend days trawling through the endless maze of hospital corridors. I had to escape. While Jack was being tested, I went down to a Wendy's hamburger joint in the basement, got a black coffee and tried to dive into a new book and the words shimmered and swam off the page. I was blind with rage. What made me maddest was that surgeon who thought he could slot in major surgery, like digging in my husband's brain to decide whether there was another cancer site, in between his travel plans. The goal was Jack's overall health and survival. Within that there could be conflicts over treatments. Would something help the cancer but make the MS worse? Diagnosis is supposed to precede treatment and cure, but what if precise diagnosis makes things worse for the health of the patient? The ace neurosurgeon was focusing on accuracy rather than overall patient welfare.

It was a no-brainer: He would have the tumor removed at Pitt, followed by radiation at OSU. And the little white spot did not turn out to be malignant.

After Dr. Otto's diagnosis and the decision to suffer surgery in Pittsburgh, Jack finally called the kids. Josh, the oldest, probably wanted to say something funny, but there was nothing funny to be said. It came out as something like, "Oh that, huh." Since he and his wife Lorraine live in Columbus, they would be available in person. Wit, the middle child, an emergency medical technician on her way to med school that fall, was on task right away asking questions about symptoms and process. She would not be able to come home or to Pittsburgh because she was madly busy moving to Maine. Charlotte, the youngest, who lived in New York City, burst into tears and hung up the phone. She was clearly shocked that things were that serious. She called me later and decided she would meet us in Pittsburgh because the ordeal would be easier to endure if she was on the scene.

The morning after my husband's head was cut up, I woke after three or four hours' sleep, willing myself to relax in between spells of wakefulness, dressed and headed out of the Hampton Inn, cracking the dawn. I assumed Charlotte was still asleep in her room, and let her be. It was Tuesday and the morning rush of buses, pedestrians and bikes was in full swing. Watching out for the bikes, I zipped up the cross street connecting Forbes and Fifth, then hoofed it up the steep Lothrop Street hill. With my full backpack, I had to lean forward to balance my weight. My legs felt great, tense and working. Reaching the Presby entrance, breathless and anxious to see my husband, I ran up the escalator to the second floor and took the elevator the rest of the way.

"Get my glasses," Jack said throatily when I entered his ICU room. He wanted his glasses. He wasn't rocking in pain. *Hallelujah.* He still had an oxygen mask, though it was smaller than the monster of the night before. The ICU nurse, still on duty after close to 12 hours, was working on weaning him off the oxygen supplement. There were no restraints on his hands. We were down to 17 material interventions. The arterial blood-pressure monitor was gone. Sixteen.

The nurse administered neurological tests: "Follow my finger with your eyes. Up. Down. Wiggle your toes. Can you feel this? This?" She was poking him in the feet. "Where are you?"

"The hospital."

"What year is it?"

"Umm… is it 2004?"

No response.

"2007?"

This was a matter for serious cogitation.

"The answer is…" Jack said in his most authoritative voice, pausing for effect, "2010."

"Good. What is your pain level on a scale of one to ten?"

"Nine."

Had he turned down medication during the night? Did no one offer him something? It seemed to me that hospitals used to bring pain meds automatically. The nurse now offered him Tylenol with or without codeine.

"Take the codeine," I said in my own authoritative voice.

The nurse told Jack he would be moved out of the ICU that morning and asked him if there was anything else he needed.

"I'd like to stay in the hospital," he said.

"You're not going anywhere," she said. "Just to a regular room." In fact, it was a room on another floor with service in between intensive care and normal hospital care.

Charlotte showed up later than I expected. "I woke up early but my arms and legs were like jelly. What did you give me? I had to go back to sleep."

"Trazadone. It's a muscle relaxant."

"A muscle relaxant! You gave me a muscle relaxant? I couldn't even get out of bed." She took stock of her dad, who was aware of her presence with eyes closed behind his glasses.

The time of Jack's move was unpredictable, so we went out to lunch. When we got back, the patient was on the new floor. The oxygen mask was gone and the quiet was palpable. Fifteen. His oxygen level, high in the 90s, which is fine, was still being monitored through the clip on his toe. They had to move it from a finger because it bothered him and he kept taking it off. Jack was never compliant. In fact, he was a bull-headed person. In this case, he was a noncompliant, bull-headed person who had little idea where he was or what he was doing.

I wanted to be counting down, but the nurses had added wraps around each leg that squeezed and released automatically to prevent coronary thrombosis. Back to 16.

That morning the *New York Times* had an article about a physicist who had decided gravity was an illusion. By that he meant that it wasn't an independent underlying law of physics as we had been taught, but a result of even more important laws of thermodynamics.

"They're talking about entropy," I said to Charlotte. "Loss of information. Loss of heat. Things getting more random. It's like cancer cells not following the rules that make a human body work."

"What does that have to do with heat? Or gravity, for that matter?"

Trying to remember, I said, "The second law of thermodynamics says that everything cools down to the same temperature, so it's all the same and there's no information."

"Of course it's information. It's information that it's all the same temperature."

"There have to be zeros and ones. If it's all one or all zero, there are no distinctions. Ergo, no information." I was making it up as I went along, not at all sure of what I was saying. "You need to know about entropy. It comes up in literature… Thomas Pynchon." That much was true.

"What you said tells me nothing about gravity."

Maybe not, I thought.

Back at the hospital, we took turns ministering to the patient. His nose was leaking pink stuff, so we continually helped him with great clouds of tissues. He had almost nothing to say but 'water'. His mouth was as parched as sandpaper. A sign above his head said *WARNING. Head and neck patient. No straws. Nothing up the nose.* We gave him sips from a paper cup, trying not to let it dribble. Because he had no leg power and was tilted up in bed to keep pressure off the head, he tended to slide down, and periodically we had to call for help to move him higher in the rumpled bed. It took two people on either side. But he was making big progress getting rid of mechanisms and tubes. Someone came in to remove the EKG suction cups. Fifteen again. Ditto the blood-pressure cuff. Fourteen. The oxygen monitor on his finger. Thirteen. And the noisy machine to monitor his vital signs. A mere dozen external machinations.

It seemed an unlikely proposition before surgery that Jack would be released within a couple of days. On Wednesday, two days after the operation, we wondered whether we were looking at weeks. Only a few days before Jack could confuse me on long-term interest rates and the permutations of the remote control. Visible improvements were taking place, but I couldn't tell what if anything much was going on behind his blue eyes. He had been moved down another notch on intensity of patient care, and was in a regular hospital room on the eighth floor. I was now familiar with the majority of floors at Presby. People in the halls asked for directions, and I could often help them out.

The IV was out. Eleven! So were the two useless IV stents from the operation. Single digits. In the afternoon he had a low fever, so they began a course of antibiotics through a new IV line. Back to ten. They took him for a CT scan of the chest to see if there was any congestion. Negative.

Jack was unenthusiastic about the transition to hospital food. A food-service worker brought a full tray of bland puréed glop, but it was not welcome. Charlotte made a spoon into an airplane to slip chicken soup and pudding into the airport. She laughed at the idea of treating her father like a toddler. At least he accepted juice, so we could now spill that down his gown as well as the water.

I needed to find a bookstore. *Let the Great World Spin* was far too sad and artsy.

Leaving the ghoulish fluorescence of the hospital and stepping out into the bright July sunshine, Charlotte reflected, "I think I've figured out the issue with gravity. If the universe is expanding from the Big Bang, matter is more and more broken up, so there's not as much pull."

I stayed silent until we found a University of Pittsburgh store. As we walked inside, she persisted, "So what do you think of my idea on gravity?"

"I think it has nothing to do with the article, and you and I don't know enough to understand what they're talking about. Matter spreading out all over the place doesn't mean gravity is an illusion."

I knew better than to criticize Charlotte, and this was harsh. Worse, it had an edge of deliberation. I wanted to nick her or graze her a little, maybe because I was tired or just tired of arguing but also with the idea that she ought to be able to take it. Without a backward glance, she turned and disappeared to another part of the store.

I went to the science section to desperately search for definitions and explanations of entropy and the second law of thermodynamics among the introductory books. I had no idea what the relationship of information and energy was, nor what that would have to do with gravitational pull. I found some entries. They didn't hang together. My understanding was getting more random and entropic as I found new concepts that might or might not be connected to the question. And what was the question anyway? Maybe these other fancy words changed it?

I sought out Charlotte, who was absorbed in art materials. If I didn't apologize, it was going to be a long afternoon. I found her. She was not in tears. A good start.

Amid the shelves of classics, I found several Pynchon books. I was disappointed that my life had gone on long enough the cult novels of my twenties have been absorbed into the canon.

"I want something by Pynchon," said Charlotte, who had so far selected some India ink, a brush and an artist's pad as well as a thick paperback.

I pulled out a thin early volume, a good introduction to the elusive writer.

"No, I want to read this one," she said, taking firm hold of *Gravity's Rainbow*, 800-pages thick.

"Nobody *wants* to read *Gravity's Rainbow*. I did after college because I had to. Everybody else in my age group was talking about it like it was the second coming of *Ulysses*. Anyway, I skipped a lot of the stuff on the Russian steppes." I think I skipped other parts, too, like the hundreds of pages on Boer massacres.

"You should try this," she said, thrusting a paperback into my hand. "It has a character named Death."

"Oh boy."

"No. It's funny. He's a bureaucrat in Discworld."

I did not ask whether the law of gravity applies in Discworld. Nor did I question the wisdom of bringing a pot of black ink into a hospital room. We went back to our eighth-floor enclosure with Pynchon and art materials for her and *Major Pettigrew's Last Stand,* a light, easy-to-digest story for me. I wasn't ready to tackle far-out fantasy when my own world had become disorganized and disorienting. We spent the rest of the afternoon sketching and reading while Jack was continually interrupted from his semi-conscious state by one hospital worker or another. Emissaries from physical therapy and occupational therapy came in separately. Why both, I did not know. Each went through the usual rigmarole of getting him to wiggle his toes and give his name.

"Who's the president?" asked one of them, with some originality.

"Reagan," Jack replied with conviction.

"Afraid not. Is it Obama?"

"Yes," with equal conviction.

"Who are those people?"

"Charlotte," said Jack, looking at me.

"And Wit," looking at Charlotte.

Charlotte and I looked at each other. I was sure she was thinking how happy we'd been to hear her father's voice after they took off the oxygen mask Monday night.

On Thursday morning I found the patient deep in a normal sleep. The catheter was out. So the magic number was nine. No leg wraps, either. Eight. The young nurse, dark-skinned and sunny with a bright smile, came in to quiz him. *He knew the year! And the month! What a genius!*

An evil thought came to me. I asked if Hillary Clinton was president.

"Yes," he said, then thought about it. "No."

I apologized. You shouldn't hit a man when he's wearing a gown.

A neurosurgical resident arrived in the afternoon to take off the bandage and drain on the posterior of the skull. Six. Then, one by one, he removed the seven staples over that wound. He took off the bloody bandage across the forehead as well. That revealed the 35 thick staples locking down the monstrous incision, like something designed by Dr. Frankenstein himself. Jack was in costume for a Halloween party. I took stock. We were down to: An IV line to deliver an antibiotic; the staples across the forehead; and the NFL lineman piece of tape across the bridge of his nose holding the strings that were attached to packing up the nasal passage.

We were going to blow this joint. The hitch was the patient was not back to normal mentally but was strong enough to get in trouble. The occupational therapists arrived and tested him pulling on a robe, then standing. He staggered forward wordlessly holding onto their arms.

"Where are you going?" they asked.

"The bathroom." He would not be stopped. They were going to help him whether or not it was in their job description.

We picked up a milkshake for Jack at McDonald's, as requested. No straw. Charlotte was disgusted that he wanted something from Mickey D's, but whatever he would eat was okay with us. We got back to the room to find the nurse in a state.

"He pulled the packing out of his nose," she huffed, exasperated.

Indeed, there they sat on his food tray, one from each nostril, like two thoroughly soaked tampons.

The nurse tightened her lips. "Why did you do it?"

"Because I was stupid," Jack said in that tone which sounded so compos mentis and that I had learned to distrust.

A resident showed up with two other doctors, fewer than usual but impressive for eight at night. "Usually we like those to stay in a week to ten days," he said morosely.

"I was stupid." Jack repeated what he'd said to the nurse. At least he was clear on that.

I was terrified. Here we were thankfully down to two obtrusive measures of medical support, yet losing ground.

The resident called Dr. Snyderman, who ordered a scan to see if anything had moved. By 'anything' he included additional surgical packing that I had not been aware of. So the magic number was actually three. All was stable, and the schedule remained the same to remove the deep packing the following Monday. The MRI came out fine. The resident said to watch for leakage of a clear liquid from a nostril. I suspected a drip would indicate a spinal fluid leak, one of the worst complications of Jack's type of surgery. By 9 p.m., I'd had it and we left.

In my hotel bed, the covers still neat on the empty side, I worried that Jack would have a nose leak and not call the nurse. He seemed to keep forgetting he had a call button. Or maybe he used it and nobody came. I knew I needed to hire a private nurse.

Early Friday, as Charlotte and I walked into the room, Jack asked us, "Can I have my BlackBerry?" Another step forward.

He flicked through his emails, and I could see both eyes were less swollen. His left forearm, where the IV line had been removed, was bruised. That left only the staples across the forehead and whatever was way up in the sinus cavity. Two.

The scuttlebutt among the nurses that morning was about transferring Jack to a rehab room, another promotion. The physical therapist got Jack into a wheelchair. Super excited, I offered a ride and trotted him down the hall to the visitors' lounge, where Charlotte was hanging out. Happy to be doing my old job, I went faster and called out to Charlotte, "Look what I have."

"Stop!" the patient wailed, sick to his stomach from the speed.

Back in the hospital room to Jack's relief, Charlotte had accumulated a number of India-ink drawings of a vase of flowers and of her dad. Sketching me wasn't as easy because, apparently, I "moved around too much."

I was ruminating again. "You know there's entropy and there's the force of life. Against disorder, there's always emerging complexity."

"What goes up must come down."

I ignored that. "Yeah. Zeroes and ones. The ones win out just a little bit. And that's where life is. And maybe God."

"Would the two of you just stop it," Jack snapped as if his pain level shot up from two to eight. "Just stop it!"

Arriving back from our lunch break, we found the nurse unhappy and harried. "He fell on the floor," she said. "I was walking by the door and there he was on the floor." He was trying to get into his wheelchair and then to the bathroom.

Charlotte looked at her father with a devilish, maternal glint in her eyes. "We can't even leave you for an hour."

We impressed upon Jack the importance of not trying to get up when no one else was around. What if he fell on his head?

"Can we get someone to be with him overnight?" I asked the nurse.

"I don't know whether the doctor will order it or not, but I can ask."

We were both politely ignoring the India-ink spill, a black lake that was swallowing up the linoleum floor and demonstrating the law of surface tension in a big way. Crouching down, Charlotte was furiously mopping it up with a great swirl of paper towels.

Dr. Snyderman, who must have been peeved at his patient's lack of compliance but also convinced that more oversight was a good idea, ordered an overnight sitter. The idea of a rehab room was scratched. Since it was already Friday, the patient could stay where he was for the weekend.

Sometime mid-afternoon the cavalry from Columbus, Josh and Lorraine, arrived in the hospital room. The nurse had a hard time elbowing herself in with the clutter of equipment and the crowd of

Davises, scattered and squeezed, all chairs occupied and Josh, a large piece of equipment himself, standing.

We'd been subsisting on student-cafeteria food for the week. Now was the chance for something better. Charlotte found us an upscale but casual restaurant for that evening.

"I love going to someplace that doesn't take reservations," I said.

"That's incredibly snooty," Charlotte mocked, "What, are you slumming?"

"I meant that with your dad we always have to plan ahead."

On our post-prandial visit to the hospital, armed with delicious macaroni and cheese for the patient, I told Jack I'd be in by seven the next morning, when the night sitter was scheduled to leave. "What are you *not* going to do?"

"Get out of bed," Jack answered dutifully.

Saturday night I pulled out the stops and booked us at Eleven, billed as one of the hottest restaurants in the city. I ignored the name that seemed either fortuitous or weird given my preoccupation with countdowns. It was clean, modern and swanky, with a hint of old-world elegance in the double-height draperies and dark hardwood walls. We were seated upstairs, another taste of freedom.

As one of us tried a glass of Portuguese wine, Charlotte reflected, "I was supposed to go to Portugal with a friend once and missed the flight. I didn't really want to go with them anyway."

"That sounds as snooty as me wanting to go somewhere they don't take reservations."

"I went to the wrong London airport."

"That doesn't help." What I really wanted to ask is whether 'them' was a 'him' them or a 'her' them, but didn't press it.

As we sipped the wine and waited for our food, the conversation turned heavy, and I found myself saying I never wanted to move from my house whatever happened. No downsizing. No assisted living. Nowhere except directly to a nursing home or the crematorium.

Lorraine, leaning her long, lithe frame toward me, said that nursing homes were lousy places and maybe I didn't mean that. I told them I had long-term care insurance and a nursing home was okay if there were visiting therapy dogs. I felt a subtle altering of relationships as we talked. Had I meant to share this information at this time? Who were these large people? We were here to take care of Jack. I don't need my children hovering. Where was Jack when I needed him? *Watch out for the kids taking charge*, I thought. *I'm the boss.*

Sunday morning Lorraine was in Jack's room before I was. He was sitting in his wheelchair complaining that no one was doing a thing about rehab.

"This is nuts," he said. He was right. If they had moved him to a rehab facility someone would be working with him. As it was, he was pretty well back to pre-operation functioning and irritable as heck. It was a relief but frustrating not to be able to do more.

Charlotte left for the airport to get back to school in New York. Josh and Lorraine took me to the National Aviary for a bit of respite. Sitting in the back seat as we drove, I again had the irksome feeling of ceding power to my children. "Thank you for taking me to see the penguins, mommy and daddy," I silently murmured to my young company.

The ground was shifting in our relationships. I wasn't sure I liked it. A decade later, I would learn to be deeply grateful and accepting of the help of my mature children, who were constantly respectful, never controlling and fully present for tough times and decisions.

Monday morning, July 19th, a week after the surgery, Dr. Snyderman showed up at Jack's door with his white-coated courtiers. He would take out the detritus from the operation that day. A resident removed the 35 staples, and the famous doctor himself undertook the nose cleaning. Jack was untethered. His heart, lungs, stomach, renal system and brain were humming. Not his leg muscles, of course, but this was good enough.

From the time the operation was planned, I envisioned returning in triumph, driving Jack's car home to Columbus with him in the passenger seat. No stops along the way. Simply a victory parade with one car. As it was, Josh chauffeured Jack in his adapted Toyota van.

"I'll drive," I said to Lorraine as the valet pulled up Josh's car. It was pre-emptive and peremptory. I was pulling rank as I know it and escaping Hospitalworld, a warren of vertical closed spaces that, like New York or Discworld or the whole bloody incomprehensible universe, runs by its own rhythms and rules.

The next morning, when Charlotte called, I told her there was a letter to the editor about the gravity article. I read it out to her, "'As the universe expands, is this not entropy? As the universe expands, would not gravity be reduced, and with it the essence of light and particles... leading to not enough 'stuff' to make anything?' And pretty darn cold, too, not that it matters."

A moment of exquisitely empty silence. "Hah," she said.

3

THE RIGHT TREATMENT

Seven years after Jack's unnerving bout with cancer of the nose it was my turn. A friend saved my life. That is a trite saying and a pretentious exaggeration unless Lassie, the genius collie in the 1950s TV show, had wrestled a rattlesnake to death when its fangs were pointed at her owner's leg as he lay disabled from a cliff fall and she had to run miles over rugged terrain to find help.

To be precise, a friend reduced the probability that breast cancer would kill me.

Marty, a woman with a short, sensible haircut like mine, offered to accompany me to the initial consultation with the surgeon. I was touched by her kindness and willingness to commit a whole day and more from her packed schedule. Marty was a busy woman with two almost-grown but not quite out-of-the-nest children. She was an active supporter of various causes, including serving as a delegate for Hillary Clinton at the 2016 Democratic Convention. A former shrink, Marty exuded an unusual combination of deep sensitivity and practicality just as deep. With her medical background, she would be able to ask questions and filter the answers intelligently, especially since I would miss key words through my staticky ears. Together we prepared a list of questions for the surgeon.

With companionship and forms to fill out, the half-hour wait whizzed by. A nurse called my name. Marty waited some more. The nurse led me to a scale. I slipped off my shoes to drop a half pound. In the examining room, I changed to a robe and perched on the table. My feet didn't reach the bench, and I wiggled each through the alphabet, waiting for the knock on the door. It could come anytime, right now or in an hour, given a surgeon's erratic schedule. They say there's nothing certain but death and taxes. Only one of those has a date on a calendar, however. To calm my nerves, I switched from the alphabet to picking at my cuticles, bloodying one.

I jumped at the sudden knock on the door. Dr. P. briskly entered, followed by a nurse. I surreptitiously licked the blood off my finger. The surgeon, with a bald pate and a chinstrap beard to make up for it, excised my history with white-coated authority.

"I have a friend with me," I managed to get in. "She's a doctor and wants to take notes."

His eyes had not yet met mine. Now he looked pissed. "What *kind* of doctor?"

"A psychiatrist. Retired."

This was a very bad answer. Two decades earlier Marty was practicing psychiatry in New York, but after the towers went down on 9/11 and a tempest of dust clouds and debris rained over the city, she reevaluated her life, moved to Columbus with her family, and quit medicine. She also started writing, which is how we met, joining a writing group together and becoming fast friends. Marty was going to have to be careful. The surgeon went from impassive to stone-faced. He was not pleased to have a kibitzer who knew little about his specialty. That was, of course, reasonable, but I was happier than before to have a friend with me who understood cells and organs, if not peanut farming.

"Lie down, please," he said in close to a monotone. "Open your robe."

I pulled the panels wide for the full reveal.

The doctor found the lump and fingered its dimensions. He prodded the rest of the left breast and my left armpit, then went methodically onto the right side. His fingers worked delicately and forcefully, a mammary virtuoso.

The nurse left to invite Marty in for the verdict. I sat up straight and kept my face impassive, a student waiting for an assignment.

The surgeon concluded the tumor was the size of a peanut. Probably at stage one, since he couldn't feel anything unusual in the lymph nodes. There was no indication it had leaked to surrounding tissue. It sounded like the solution was a lumpectomy to dig the thing out, or at most a single mastectomy to remove the rest of an asset that wasn't of obvious value to a 71-year-old.

"Doctor," said Marty, "Vivian is Jewish. Shouldn't she have genetic testing?"

The hand-written form where I'd checked off my heritage on my very first visit, the one for the mammography, hadn't made it to the surgeon. I knew the question was important, but not why. It's because people of Ashkenazi Jewish descent, which includes most American Jews, are susceptible to genetic mutations called BRCA-1 and BRCA-2 that make breast cancer more likely.

The surgeon's lips tightened. He'd been called out. "She'll need a referral to a genetic counselor," he said, and arranged it.

Marty and I debriefed over tea in the so-called brasserie downstairs. Not a warm person, we agreed. I recalled Dr. A, who wanted to conduct a ten-hour surgical biopsy of my husband's brain back in 2010. Many surgeons have tremendous egos. They are godlike interventionists, short on time or natural inclination to delve into the patient's thoughts and feelings.

"On the other hand," Marty reflected, "he appeared completely competent."

The geneticist, our next call, had "a sprinkling of empathy," as Marty put it. She drew helpful if/then diagrams with probabilities and outcomes. She photocopied academic articles for me. I'm a garden-variety social scientist and the structure and methods were familiar, though bristling with endless Latinate vocabulary. You get an education you don't want when you come down with a nasty disease. Nonetheless, information is medicine: it gives the illusion of control.

Summing up, the geneticist remarked that the cancer was triple negative.

That sounded positive. Obviously, the tumor was lacking something deadly. My brain grasped for any scrap of hope it could find. "What does that mean?"

The geneticist, treading delicately, lowered her eyes and said, "It tells us what kind of medications we need to give you."

Marty, staring ahead sphinxlike, didn't say anything.

Smelling evasiveness, once home, I Googled triple-negative breast cancer. The lump tested negative for estrogen receptors, progesterone receptors and the HER2 protein. Thus, the usual hormonal chemotherapy wouldn't work. There were alternative drugs, but overall the malignancy was more aggressive and the five-year survival rate lower.

Mystery solved. Whoopee.

The genetic testing, which stamped my Jewish heritage on my identity like a passport, came back positive for the BRCA-2 anomaly. A malignant lump with three negatives and ancestral revenge, like those TV mysteries where hundreds of years ago someone had a grudge. Negative for certainty. Negative for avoiding the demeaning indignities of illness and age like those mercilessly inflicted on my spouse. Negative for seeing my grandson grow into the man he was meant to be.

The choice was a lumpectomy or a double mastectomy, proclaimed Dr. P. I'd been counting on the former, losing one breast rather than having my whole chest cut off. That wasn't on the table. Taking off the affected left breast wouldn't solve the problem of risk to the right one. A lumpectomy would require extra watching, terrified every day at what I might find as the warm shower water rained down. Given the risks of recurrence in either the ipsilateral or contralateral breast (herein lies a vocabulary lesson), it came down to a double or nothing proposition. I agreed to the safest route. Surgery would be followed by several months of chemo, completed a few weeks before Christmas.

In the dark September morning hours, Josh, as good a driver as his dad, ferried me in his red Subaru to the James Cancer Hospital at Ohio State to be filleted. I bade goodbye to my round friends the evening before in front of the bathroom mirror. I hefted them with my hands, admiring the perky nipples and dark aureoles. I thought about taking a photograph so I could remember them, but figured that was wacko, especially given how photos can travel. It would hardly be something to post to my Facebook page. "Those breasts are flat and fallen now," wrote Yeats. "Those veins must soon be dry." Mine still looked ambitious and optimistic to me. Too bad the left one already harbored destruction, the right one wasn't going to be good at defending itself, and the rest of my organs were fair game.

On our way to the hospital, I tried to focus on getting the ordeal over with. I was supposed to be strong with my son, but slipped up. The fear struck me with the full force of a speeding train. My eyes welled up and I crumbled at the thought about being cut up. "Just take me home now. I'm going to skip this." It wasn't a joke. It was a whimper.

Josh stared straight ahead and kept driving in silence. Like his father, he didn't go in for displays of feeling.

Get me out of this nightmare. Press the snore button, Jack, and wake me up.

At the ungodly hour of 5:30 a.m., the long underground hall-ways leading from the hospital garage to the cavernous lobby were quiet as a rural graveyard that no one visits. We found the wait-ing room, already populated. Waited. I'd brought a book, but was too numb and sleepy to open it. This time it was a slim, soothing Jacqueline Winspear mystery of a spirited female detective who solves yet another crime. The minutes ticked by until my name was called. Josh helped me to register, making sure I heard instructions correctly, and came along as we obediently followed a hospital staffer along long white hallways and into the pre-op room, where I was assaulted by astringent smells. People in uniform prodded me, checking my vitals. A nurse poked in an IV. The surgeon arrived with a heavy metal box carrying radioactive dye that he shot into me to light up the lymph nodes. At 8 a.m., I turned my hearing aids and glasses over to Josh, and the orderlies rolled me out to the corridor, made several confusing 90-degree turns and arrived in a shockingly bright oper-ating room that smelled even more of that kind of clean that covers up who knows what. Half a dozen people dressed for space travel in white and blue were busily engaged in mysterious preparations. The good doctor yelled in my right ear to move onto the operating table, and positioned me there for the mammary excision.

"I'm sorry you have to shout, doctor," I said and woke up in the recovery room. It was like waking up after a car crash: everything hurt.

The following day, they sent me home. I slowly sank onto my back in my half of the split bed. The Japanese maple, still in full leaf in all its vivid burgundy glory, brushed against the open bedroom window in a gentle late-summer breeze. I am a side sleeper, but even trying to lay my wounded body on its side a blast of pain shot across my chest. It would be many weeks before I tried that again. My chest was on fire and I could barely move without wincing. I wondered whether it was really good practice to send a patient home the day after the slicing and dicing of a double mastectomy. That morning I had walked round and round the cavernous corridors of the recovery floor trying to encourage my bladder. Being able to pee was my ticket home. I suspect the hospital staff was eager to get everyone possible out of there. Not only was it Saturday, but there was a home Ohio State football game that afternoon. The staff would want to watch on TV, and the university campus would be a crowded parking lot.

It was a relief to have the dissection part of my adventure over, but my lungs were crushed by what felt like a continuous mammogram. I assumed part of the pain came from a tightly wrapped bandage but couldn't tell exactly how or where. Five surgical drains, two on the right side and three on the left, hung out of my sides on flexible, 18-inch-long tubes, the clear-plastic collection bags attached to my floral pajama bottoms with safety pins. Their job was to draw out fluid. The drains were labeled DAVOL, presumably the company that made them. I named them Daphne, Althea, Violet, Ophelia and Leda. The dour surgeon had impressed on me that I was not to move my arms up more than 45-degrees high. This would encourage the volume of fluid to decline to the point where the drains could be removed. I wore Jack's polo shirts, so large that I didn't have to lift my arms much to get them on. As soon as I was able, I ordered button-up blouses online from Talbots.

Tests confirmed a stage-one malignancy. Excellent news for a change. The surgeon had excised the lymph nodes in my left armpit, not because they were compromised, but because the dye injected to seek out cancer hadn't trickled into every node. He was playing it safe, exactly as he should. Because the tumor was at an angle on the left breast, the surgeon had to cut diagonally, including clipping a bit of muscle to achieve the margins he wanted. He asked me ahead of time if I wanted the right breast to be cut horizontally or mirror the other side. I chose the latter since it would look better, though who was going to see that fearful symmetry?

I looked forward to the next dose of oxycodone as if it were a Friday-night martini after a tough work week. I held my heavy analogue alarm clock at an uncomfortable angle with my left hand and the savior pill in my right as I supplicated the snail of a minute hand to tick faster. After a few days, I graduated from oxycodone to Percocet, another opiate drug, because the dim-wittedness began to seem worse than the pain. Jack was fully cared for and went about his truncated life. Floating aimlessly in my druggy haze, I felt like I was on vacation. I had no responsibilities.

I knew how much better off I was than many cancer patients. I remembered a woman in a wheelchair waiting for her ride outside the Spielman Center. We exchanged looks, and I could see she was tired, ill and sad. I didn't know her circumstances, but the odds were that not only was she sicker but didn't benefit from the same level of social and material capital. There were women who had to travel for hours to get to daily chemo treatments. Women who were taking care of children. Women who had jobs they couldn't let go of however weak and unwell. Women who didn't have health insurance or for whom even copays were hard to come up with. Women whose husbands assumed their wives were going to take care of them while sick. And women who ignored their symptoms until it was too late because their jobs as wives, mothers and earners came first.

A couple of days after surgery, my brother Donnie and his wife Lisal came to visit, bearing homemade chocolates and looking serious. We sat in the bedroom, I on the cedar chest in front of the bed, and they in chairs facing me. Warm September light streamed through the windows. Steve was helping Jack with his breakfast downstairs, a blueberry granola from Whole Foods that he liked to linger over. I was dressed for the occasion in a bright, buttonless blue top with a delicate Indian-inspired pattern of white stitching. I had painfully pulled it over my head at far more than 45 degrees. It did nothing to hide the flatness. The drains hung below the shirt in full view. I could see myself sitting there, aware of the picture I made, but I was well-drugged and it was family, so I didn't mind.

Donnie was calm and focused. Lisal, an elegant, bejeweled woman with skin she somehow kept smooth as a debutante, unlike me, was similarly serene. I am wrinkled from years of foolish sun exposure. She was the hostess with the mostest, the one who puts parties together, such as a baby shower when Lorraine had Vincent and an annual family Christmas dinner. Donnie was quiet, exuding empathy. Lisal chattered on neutral topics, sending the message 'we're with you on this'.

4

GOODBYE OPHELIA

Slowly recovering, I hired extra aides for 24/7 care, often a woman overlapping with Steve who would focus on me. Rachael turned out to be a huge boon. We became friends who shared cuttings of interesting succulents to replant. One night Jack and I watched a racier show than our usual murder mysteries and detective series. It was a mini-series on sex trafficking in Australia.

Rachael, whose husband was a pastor, looked shocked.

"It's okay," I said. "The producer is a woman, and she's criticizing it, not exploiting it."

She kept watching with wide-eyed interest.

Rachael, who looked far too young to be a grandmother, shared photographs of her new baby granddaughter every week. She proved to be not only a sharp-eyed caregiver but a jigsaw-puzzle whiz. Bending her long frame over the 1,998-piece puzzle of Escher-like complexity that I had foolishly bought, she clicked pieces into place with the same rhythm and attention she devoted to dressing Jack. She finished it, except for the two that fell on the floor and Ari, the puppy, ate.

With the help of Steve, Rachael and a few others, Jack's needs were taken care of day and night, to my great relief. "The patient in bed 101 needs a drink of water," I'd say through the baby monitor, and someone would show up. The joke made Jack break up with joyful laughs.

Steve's physical therapy for his patient included throwing a pillow back and forth as Jack was tilted up in bed. Once upon a time it had been a six-pound ball at the gym, then a four-pound ball, and now a pillow at home.

Jack threw the pillow to him at the end of the bed.

"What kind of care do I give you?" Steve asked. It was one of their running jokes.

"Excellent quality care," Jack would say, trying not to crack up. If he failed the test, Steve might hurl the heap of feathers at his chest full blast.

From lovers and companions, Jack and I were reduced to roommates. Cuddling was even more essential, and now we were denied that. I told myself I wasn't neglecting my husband. After all, I was right there. And I shouldn't feel neglected myself. He did his best.

Like many of my boomer generation, the defining events of Jack's youth and mine were the civil rights and women's rights movements and the Vietnam War. As the bloodshed in Vietnam raged on, the violence and resistance at home swelled too. Many young people were deeply politicized. Some of us became involved in politics to make the world a better place. The summer of 1970, Jack and I both found work on the Ohio gubernatorial campaign of the anti-war, pro-rights John 'Jack' Gilligan. A charismatic Irish Catholic with their common gift of words, Gilligan sounded like a Kennedy and looked like a Kennedy, thus attracting national attention. While I was drafting press releases and speeches, the campaign scheduler would wander in to report on how he'd figured out how to get the candidate six different places in all corners of the state for one day of appearances from dawn until dusk. The scheduler was Jack, and, despite the logistical potential of his proposals, the candidate would shoot down half of them on the basis of personal survival. I was dating another guy and didn't think much of Jack and his office wall covered with yellow, legal-pad sheets of paper for every day of the campaign, filled with penciled ideas and offers of engagements for Jack G.

Our man won. After the campaign, I broke up with my boyfriend, remaining close friends ever since, and Jack and I went to work in the administration. I started in the welfare department, and later had the great good luck of becoming a policy analyst at the brand-new state Environmental Protection Agency. Jack headed to the personnel department, trying to fire Republicans and replace them with our sort. The following summer of '71, we drifted together through mutual friends. Suddenly, the second time around, I noticed those blue eyes, as clear and sparkling as sea glass. He was funny and sensitive, exactly the type of guy I had fallen for more than once.

Now decades later, things I was glad for as I recovered from surgery were giving Jack light kisses on the lips, eating, petting the dogs, reading in bed and having Percocet handy.

Things I wished I could do: floss my teeth, shave my legs, lift my dogs, wash my hair, lift a glass or coffee cup down from a cabinet, go out to dinner. Not have drains in my chest.

Through a Percocet mist, I clicked up the handwritten daily record of the amount of fluid in each drain onto an Excel spreadsheet. The numbers weren't falling. The surgeon didn't waste a glance at the spreadsheet, sticking to the penciled record.

"You've been doing too much," he said in an accusing tone, without looking up. "Drains don't lie."

Like a scolded schoolkid caught cheating, I held my lips together tight.

"You've had *major* surgery," he added pointedly. Though the surgeon still didn't look me in the eyes, it was by far the greatest emotion he had shown.

He unwrapped the boa constrictor bandage from my chest but left all five sucking sisters in place. He moved the beginning of chemo back a week from the original schedule, saying I needed more time to recover. I would have to get better before they poisoned me.

With the bandage removed, I could have taken a look at the spaces my breasts had occupied. I didn't want to. I avoided the mirror, but in a shower it was harder to miss the sight. The hospital had issued a flimsy bralette, less supportive than a 12-year-old's training bra. When I slid it up over my head and the two gauze pads fell to the floor, a sideways glance willy-nilly picked up the raw diagonal scars. A woman's most obvious jewelry was gone.

After a few days of druggy denial, I realized it was important that I look at my chest to make sure there was no infection. I faced the bathroom mirror unshielded. I was repulsive. That medieval sicko Hieronymus Bosch was messing with me. My chest resembled one of the freakish creatures and floating severed body parts of his ghoulish paintings. But I would be the sicko if I didn't face the facts. I forced a squeamish second look, wincing. The meaninglessly symmetrical diagonal gashes were bright red but not angry looking, an engineering feat of 21st-century medicine. I had thought of breast surgery as 'going flat', but the pectoral muscles above and below formed a rim enclosing two concave circles that looked like volcano craters, with the exception of the small break where the surgeon removed a bit of muscle.

I was unwilling to mourn what I'd lost: my breasts, my hair, my strength. But it had cut deeper than I was able to admit. I had to get used to a strange new body. On one of my early appointments, which I thought was just with the surgeon, I was shuttled up after that to visit a plastic surgeon, a young Asian-American fellow. Flicking through a tablet with the earnest intensity of a car salesman, he showed me photographs of various reconstruction techniques. I sat on the examining table looking at the palm-sized saline implants and silicone implants. He explained that 'gummy bear' implants are so named because the form stays stable even when the shell holding them is broken. He clicked through a sequence of photos showing the stages of inserting liquid implants that start as boob buds and grow to a size that a swimwear model or porn star would be proud to flaunt.

It was like a cartoon book where the figure changes as you flip quickly through. I didn't want to be impolite to the young doctor, but had a giddy urge to giggle. He went on to depictions of nipple additions and aureoles tattooed to look normal. Did I want clip-on or bolt-on hubcaps? My body was shaking with laughter, and I hoped he thought it was some other emotion.

I politely declined remodeling. It would require two more surgeries and a form of fakery I didn't want. Instead I would get silicone pads that slipped into a specially designed bra, also fakery, but far less intrusive.

Thinking of fakery, I remembered the summer after I turned 12 in 1958. My family was visiting Char's parents' house in Columbus. Grandparents, parents, siblings and cousins gathered for an alfresco lunch at the long wooden table in a clearing near a sweeping lawn. I was wearing a polo shirt that was a bit tight. Dick, noticing my snug shirt, said, "You're becoming a sweater girl." I was embarrassed but now remember it as a sweet way to say what was happening.

Secretly I tried on a stretchy dress, stuffed in two tennis balls, and tried to visualize the woman I was becoming. My breasts never grew to be much larger than tennis balls, but they filled out clothes and tickled me with dreams of romance. Jack adored them. And all my earlier guys, when I was dating, made it clear they found them perfectly formed.

A crone is a woman who has passed menopause. What is a woman with no uterus and no breasts? A super crone? I had had a hysterectomy decades ago for menopausal reasons, and of course it wasn't noticeable, but if I was scoring up my physical femininity it counts. I'd never wanted to be feminine in the sense of meek deferral to a limited role. Nor had I wanted to be a feminist who burns her bras and matronizes the opposite sex. Now I mourned the status of incomplete woman. Mourning is regret, I told myself, not the same as feeling sorry for yourself. Rachael brought in nail polish and gave me a mani-pedi in a vivid, vampish red by OPI called 'My Chihuahua Bites'. They didn't carry 'My Pomeranian Nips'.

As women age, they wear more make-up and jewelry, and the maintenance itself becomes a part-time job. That's what my ladies' tennis team was doing with the large zirconium earrings (the diamond ones left safely at home), the Lilly Pulitzer tennis dresses and the colored hair refreshed every few weeks before the roots begin to show. I looked at my honest white hair in the mirror and wondered what it was going to be like to lose it during chemo. The medications to stop rapidly growing cancer cells in their tracks also disrupt rapidly growing hair cells. My head would advertise my condition.

I focused more on recovering, determinedly imagining my arms were in a straitjacket and looking forward to the next visit to the surgeon as for absolution from a crime.

"Take a deep breath," Dr. P. instructed and started a steady yank. I felt one invasive tapeworm in my chest cavity sliding through my innards. The deep breath didn't help much. He pulled out another. The pain was in a way desirable, like the pleasure a child gets from wiggling out a baby tooth. Daphne and Leda, including the foot-long length from inside my body, were no more.

"Next time, take some Percocet before you come in," a nurse told me afterwards.

"Can I ease up on the restrictions?" I asked as Violet and Althea waved goodbye the following week, this time with the pain blocked by strong drugs.

He shot me a disapproving look. "What do you think I'm going to say?"

While the good doctor was out of the room, I appealed to a nurse. "He's strict," she said. "But he gets good results with a lower rate of post-operative infection." I wondered whether the doctor had experienced rebellious or noncompliant patients who got into real trouble.

Ophelia, naturally, was the last to go singing down a stream on Tuesday, October 3rd. It had taken a month, but in the first set of the treatment program, I was victorious.

"Goodbye, young lady," said the doctor, shaking my hand and looking almost friendly. The appellation could be taken as demeaning. Would he say "goodbye, young man" to a male patient? Not that he had many, if any. I couldn't help liking 'young lady' anyway.

Now I could lie on my side to sleep. I didn't have to wear boring button-down blouses, though I had acquired quite a collection in bright fall plaids. It was a win-win all around.

5

CODDLED AND POISONED

Once again into the breach. The elm tree over the driveway was beginning its annual shedding. Steve brushed away the brown leaves from the van's windshield in the pre-dawn darkness before Jack and I boarded. Early in October we were headed to the James Cancer Hospital for installation of a port below my clavicle through which to infuse nasty chemicals and withdraw necessary blood samples. In consultation with Wit, our daughter and genuine family doctor, that seemed simpler than sticking me with a needle all the time. My veins have been known to be difficult to locate, and I hate the nurses dowsing at likely spots before they finally find a way in.

Who knew how much of a procedure inserting a port would be? It was a bit of surgery in itself. Strip from the waist up. Wear a gown. This one tied in back, which seemed odd. Wait. Be interviewed by innumerable tech people and nurses. Wait. Meet the anesthesiologist. Meet the doctor who will dig the hole. Wait. Be wheeled into the scalpel-bright OR, my whole body freezing. Transferred to a sitting position in what was like a dentist's chair made for space travel. Warm blankets added, thank goodness.

Beneath glaring white lights, Dr. Spain, the supervising doc, read off the steps of the procedure to his team in a far corner of the room. I heard the discussion, since they hadn't needed to take away my hearing aids. I wondered whether the doctor was indeed from Spain, and, if so, from Catalonia, and sending money to the movement for independence from the central government. I attended a lecture on that a few months before.

"Okay," I said.

"I'm not talking to you."

"Oh. I thought it was one more checklist."

Ignoring me, he read again. "Port on left or right?"

"The right," I shouted across the room. The idea was to protect the recovering tumor site and the missing lymph nodes under my left arm.

Moments later, as I was splayed against the surgical dentist's chair to be carved open, through the 'conscious sedation' I heard a male doctor quietly instruct a female one on how to thread the line through my jugular vein. "A little more to the left. That's good," he'd said. "Take it slowly…"

Wit told me later I wasn't supposed to be able to hear and recall such a discussion. Luckily, I was too sedated to be bothered that someone was practicing on my jugular vein like a coach trying to get a player to serve to the opponent's backhand: "Point your left foot this way."

Someone wheeled me back to the room where I'd started. Jack and Steve had gone home. It was a relief and something of a surprise to see Josh and Vincent waiting for me. The funny thing about coming out of surgery is you have no sense of time passing. I emerged weakened and needed time not only to recover from the anesthesia but the shock of realizing I had just listened to people matter-of-factly cutting a slot into my already chopped-up chest. Looking at my cheerful and happily untroubled grandson sparked a smile and a muted but familiar dopamine rush.

A nurse came in to check me out. The patient seemed alert. Pulse and blood pressure were fine. Afterwards she said, "If you'd like something to eat, that's okay. Something simple like crackers and juice." She looked at Josh. "There's a vending machine down the hall."

Josh and Vincent came back with cheese-and-cracker sandwiches and apple juice for grandmother and grandson. Both of us sucked eagerly on our straws. Never has apple juice tasted sweeter nor cheese and crackers as satisfyingly salty.

With my itchy, painful port in place, the medical establishment deemed me ready for the first chemotherapy session at the Spielman Center in mid-October. All my appointments seemed to be at the crack the dawn. My friend Jody drove me to the breast-cancer factory at 7:45 a.m. She was a former captain of my New Albany tennis team who had the sense to recognize when she wasn't able to play as well as she wanted and quit for other pursuits. Jody came down with breast cancer a couple of years before me and was assigned the same oncologist. She sailed through the treatments, which was reassuring. Jody was the ideal companion for a day where I didn't know what to expect. Once again, I had the luck to have a friend who would do more than keep me company. A calm person, with dark, short hair rather like Marty's—the retired shrink and nascent writer who helped me through surgery—Jody methodically reviewed the treatment steps as we drove.

Everything a breast-cancer patient could possibly need was right there at the Spielman Center. The website described it as having 'a spa-like feel', and it was as soothing as such a place could possibly be. Every employee I dealt with, from the receptionists to the doctors, seemed focused on me, the hurting person in front of them.

Stefanie Spielman was the wife of Ohio State football star Chris Spielman, who played in the NFL for the Detroit Lions and other teams. She developed breast cancer young, way too young. The Spielmans raised millions for breast-cancer research at Ohio State. Stephanie took on the cause with energy and effectiveness, creating a support group for young women with the disease, hosting an annual cancer-survivor event, and funding low-income patients and their families. Her death at the age of 42 at her home in Upper Arlington was mourned by the entire community.

In the third-floor examining room, Jody had a reunion with the nurses, hugging her old friends. She sat patiently as nurses and study investigators quizzed me. Several different researchers had asked me to be a subject for their studies. There had to be a sea of research funding for breast cancer. Research for me is like a Chinese banquet, and I didn't hesitate to sign up for a double-blind test of a medication they thought might reduce cognitive fuzziness or 'chemo brain', as well as a test of the impact of physical activity on markers of brain aging. For the latter, I got to wear a Fitbit to track my steps and could keep it after the study was completed. This was a no-brainer. I would want to walk as much as possible anyway. The research would require several extra vials of blood at each treatment, but the port would deliver it painlessly.

The room was now jammed tight with eight or ten women, because each investigator had at least one assistant. I consider myself an introvert who shrinks from being the center of attention, but took it like a leading lady. I didn't feel as good about being the cynosure in the coming weeks, when I had to talk about the intimate side effects of chemo to an audience. Constipation wasn't in any of my old presentation notes.

Freebies fell from the sky throughout my treatments. Small perks, like a zippered Ohio State bag, stuffed with a hand-sewn quilt made in some caring ladies' club. Free snacks sat on the chemo waiting-room counter, along with a coffee machine and bottles of water, and a basket overflowing with hats, knitted no doubt by another ladies' group. I imagined the kind women getting together to sew or knit and chat, feeling good that they could help. On my next visits, I would use the Pink Ribbon Girls for free transportation to and from chemo. Volunteer drivers used their own cars to shepherd the needy to treatment. My need was for conversation, not a free ride, and I was glad for the company. Once done with chemo, I would receive five free massages, scheduled any time I wanted, a free pair of prostheses every two years and four new bras every single year. Why Medicare should pay for free bras for me, who shopped for clothes whenever I wanted, wasn't clear. I sent checks to all the helpful groups I could identify.

I was a privileged patient. Sick, yes, but blessed with excellent quality care, which I'd gladly admit to even if Steve weren't threatening me with a pillow. I had friends who were knowledgeable and shockingly generous with their time. I could walk through the doors of a relatively intimate, freestanding institution staffed with doctors and nurses skilled and up-to-date and supported from the orderlies on up. A whole research community was interested in my disease. And gaggles of volunteers and philanthropists who heard 'breast cancer' responded with a Pavlovian desire to toss money at me through private and public channels.

I wondered whether I should feel guilty.

In a graduate finance course long ago, my professor, an older fellow and economist, railed against a federal program that attempted to allocate kidneys to those who most needed them. He said that an older person in renal failure should be allowed to die. Ironically, a few years later I ran into the professor at the OSU faculty club, and in a quiet voice he talked about the several ways he was using his intellect to hunt for a good number on the list for kidney transplants. He was desperate for a new kidney.

Thinking about the professor, I knew where his beliefs started and where they ended up. A clear-headed analysis of society's value for treating me for breast cancer would knock this lady way down the list.

The 'person years of life' lost by an adult victim of breast cancer is in the teens, according to the American Childhood Cancer Association. All that time, they will receive federal social-security payments. A kid who dies of any type of cancer will miss out on close to 70 productive years.

I had a well-advertised, well-funded disease that wasn't as dangerous as it used to be. The five-year survival rate for breast cancer in the early Nineties was 50-50. Now, depending on the type of cancer and time of diagnosis, it was in the 90 percent range. It was only the sixth most common cause of death for women. In the first quarter of the 21st century, lung cancer caused more misery and drew an eighth of the dollars directed to breast cancer. It's not a perfect world, but my age group quite possibly has collected more bennies than it deserves if you want to build an equitable economy and a society. There was no way, however, to calculate how I might be taking something away from a college student with lung cancer or a single mom who couldn't afford decent childcare, making it harder for her kid to get to college at all. I wanted to be in that 90 percent that got through five years. Then I wanted ten years more, maybe 20. I wanted to see Vincent graduate from high school and college and, hey, maybe make me a great-grandmother.

When it's down to your own game plan, to hell with the greater good.

For that first day of chemo, the powers that be installed me in a cheery, light-filled corner room with windows on two sides. I looked down on a freeway and, just by it, a busy road. Altogether it was some 12 lanes. The cars and trucks had somewhere to get to and sailed calmly on, as Auden would put it. The sun shone as it had to. As I undressed and donned my fluffy, spa-like cotton robe, I was anxious but felt cared for. The bed was as comfortable as one at the Hyatt or the Ritz, with a mountain of blankets right out of a heater. A nurse handed me a menu, in case I wanted to order food or drink during the treatment. While Jody took a break to head to the nearby bookstore, I filled out pages and pages of forms for the research studies before the nurse hooked me up to the meds that would target my cancer, Docetaxel and Cyclophosphamide. The patient education handout said the former came naturally from yew trees, which sounded soothing. The side effects listed for both was daunting, and I had refrained from learning more online. I was worried enough already.

One of the drugs contained alcohol, and with Benadryl in the IV line as well, I drifted in and out of sleep for the hour and a half or so of the infusion. Before I left, a nurse taped a drug delivery system to my belly. It would prick me exactly 27 hours later, saving a trip back to the hospital. I'd seen an ad for the device on TV during the evening news when they bombard old people with the latest treatments for the pantheon of illnesses we are heir to. Jack and I used to laugh at those.

The anti-nausea drug they sent me home with worked, and they'd loaded me with steroids to get through the first few days. The toxins would build up from treatment to treatment, making me sicker after each. There were three more chemo sessions to go. Mary, my aunt and the former tennis maven, visited and as ever, was chatty and in good spirits. We talked about the outlook for the Buckeyes, Ohio State's football team. We talked about shared philanthropic interests, like the latest challenges to and assaults on Ohio's Planned Parenthood clinics by the courts, states and federal government. We talked politics, unavoidably growing animated and angry at the antics of Donald Trump. It was early in his tempestuous four-year term, and every day brought a new outrage with no end in sight. A conversation with Mary was always infinitely various, however. It didn't need to be about the end of democracy. I'd have had to be a lot sicker not to delight in the company of someone whom age had no way of withering.

I was able to walk Russell and Ari in the neighborhood, though my chest still felt constricted when I picked up the pace, as if the stitches were too tight and about to burst. Charlotte and I talked on the phone, mainly on general topics. Wit, my middle child who made a living saving sick people, called for check-ups and to oversee every aspect of my treatment. On one call I anxiously told her blood tests showed my hemoglobin dropping down to eight g/dL. "That's not so bad," she said. "We don't get excited unless it's down to seven." That was reassuring until I remembered she was talking about getting excited in the emergency room.

Cancer is supposed to eat you up. Skeletal weight loss was a scary side effect I was determined to avoid, but I didn't account for being on steroids that goosed up appetite. And the anti-nausea drug worked fine. Jack stared in disbelief as I consumed a couple of quarts of popcorn while watching a single Ohio State football game. The chef at New Albany, Kent Rigsby, was a brilliant creator of elaborate and delicious dishes, especially Italian ones. At the club for dinner, I eschewed all that, and took to ordering New York strips that were not just rare, but blue. I attacked every ounce, though in healthier times most would need to be boxed up. If there had been raw liver in the refrigerator, I might have consumed that, too, like Mia Farrow in *Rosemary's Baby*.

During one of my chemo treatments, I ordered a Reuben sandwich and scarfed down the entire thing while the meds dripped in my arm. Usually half would be plenty. I put on two or three pounds over the course of chemo. Not a lot, but think about it. That was a *net* gain.

6

DOWN BUT NOT OUT

You pick yourself up so they can knock you down. After the next chemo treatment, the second of four, with the last scheduled three weeks before Christmas, the combination of steroids and weakness did me in. Sick and wired were a mean combination. My body was twitching, making sleep a distant dream. The site of the port had turned an ugly red around the edges. I worried that the novice surgeon had messed up but decided to wait and see if the wound got better. It did slowly, over a week. I called the doctor's office to ask for a sleep aid, but the only one approved for chemo wasn't allowed for people as old as I. With my primary-care physician, I worked out an alternative: Trazadone, the muscle relaxant and anti-depressant that helped me sleep when Jack had his nose surgery back in 2010 and made Charlotte so weak she couldn't get out of bed.

In the bathtub, bunches of my short hair came out into my hands as I rubbed in shampoo. Sitting in the water, I resisted for a minute, then maniacally started pulling out hair the way you scratch a scab. The tub looked like the aftermath of sheep shearing in the Highlands. When I emerged, I looked in the bathroom mirror to face the damage. My head was a patchy field of scrub brush. The shadowy crescent moons beneath my tired eyes looked blacker and my thick, dark eyebrows were intact and looked even darker, which was fine. Otherwise, it was difficult to recognize the old, bald woman reflected at what felt like me.

I had a flashback of my hair as a teenager when I was meeting my parents in New York. They were staying at the Plaza in February 1964. I was between semesters in my freshman year of college. I didn't stay at the Plaza myself, but at the apartment of friends. In the hotel room, Char took one look at my wild, Medusa-like head and reached for the phone. "It's an emergency," she said to her hairdresser, and off I went to be shorn. By the time I walked back from the beauty parlor, it was dark and the hotel was blocked by a swarm of teenagers. I had to push my way through the crush of policemen on foot, policemen on handsome bay horses and thousands of adolescent girls in a state of Dionysian ecstasy. They surrounded the Pulitzer Fountain and its statue of Pomona, the Roman goddess of plenty. A burly officer at first barred me from the hotel door. My eyes faced his belt buckle. I looked up, young and scared, and he let me pass. I was exquisitely groomed, quite chicly disguised as an adult, but teenage girls were persons of interest. The hysterical throngs were hoping for a glimpse of the Beatles, expected to arrive at the Plaza any thrilling minute. It was the group's first American tour. Their famous introduction to the American audience on *The Ed Sullivan Show* would be aired a couple days later, on Sunday night.

Now, many decades later, looking at my patchy scrub of hair was depressing. I knew what I had to do. My hairdresser paid a house call and shaved my head to a short and spiky buzz cut to even it out. In the mirror, the baldness now looked like someone undergoing cancer treatment. Whaddaya know. It was discouraging but the right step. I took comfort in adapting without resorting to tears or screams.

I was now navigating the wilderness that lies between the sick and well. Fitbit at the ready, I walked, first on the streets near the house, Poms on their leads, then farther afield, only Russell, the larger Pom, accompanying me. Ari was too short to go far. The daily steps ticked up. A to-do item under control.

As I took Russell on a longer walk, my sister Babette called to check in.

"How are you doing, Wiv?" she asked, using a nickname she came up with when I was running for student council president in high school: 'Win with Wiv' was her proposed slogan. "What can I get for you?"

"A hat."

The word spread through texts and emails that I needed hats, and they poured in. I developed a hat supply that would last until I turned 100, in case that was my lot. I imagined somewhere in the future Vincent's son, my great-grandson, would ask him, "Where did you get that Yankee hat that looks like R2-D2?"

It was late-fall and the mornings were cool, so hats hiding the blazing sign that said 'in cancer treatment' didn't look too bad even inside. If my hair didn't grow back until hot weather, head coverage would look odder. In the mirror, I contemplated the skull beneath the hair and tried smiling a wrinkled smile. Maybe a shorn head was a fashion statement.

"What can I do for you?" asked my next-door neighbor.

"We could use some meals," I answered boldly. It was true. One thing Steve did not do, maybe the only thing, was cook. He seemed to live on bread, cookies and burgers.

The neighbor, Peggy, organized scheduled home-cooked dinners about once a week. I looked forward to each of them for days ahead. They were full, healthy meals. Roasted chicken, corn, pastas, casseroles, stews. All comfort foods. Marty delivered two dinners, which I devoured with the hunger of a steroid-packed pro on tour. Jack and Steve were happy, too.

Friends visited often. One brought hyacinth bulbs that would bloom in the spring. They were optimism in a hard case, the opposite of my rotten peanut. Thoughtful cards and emails flooded in from good friends and from people I scarcely knew. The window washer's wife sent a lovely note. Rachael gave me a small zippered bag that said, 'Just when the caterpillar thought the world was over, it became a butterfly'. My neighbor Carole's granddaughter found a rock, painted it white and inscribed 'Be Brave' in black childish scrawl. I put it on the breakfast table, right in front of my placemat, so I'd see it every morning. In ordinary times, or when I was younger, I would have found it all sappy and sentimental. My brother Bobby and his wife Linda not only brought food but cheerily cooked dinner in our kitchen. I was touched to the core, meaning I felt all the gifts, every phone call and every flower as hugs of compassion and kindness.

And, of course, the Poms provided continual doses of comfort and reassurance.

It was Charlotte who got Jack and me started on Pomeranians. "All I want is a dog. Nothing else. Nothing," she said, approaching her 16th birthday and used to getting her way with her parents. What she really wanted was a cat, but Jack claimed to be allergic to them. Being resourceful, Charlotte went on the American Kennel Club website to search for a breed that was as much like a cat as possible. She found what she was looking for and, in her subtle way, began to ply me with offhand remarks like "Pomeranians are exceptionally trainable" and "16 is one of the most important birthdays of all."

"No, forget it. No way." I was adamant. "You'll be going away to college in two years, and we don't need the responsibility of another animal. We already have a dog." It was simple. Hobbes, the aging golden retriever, full name Hobbes Descartes, was enough trouble for the aging parents.

Jack and I stuck with our decision with no regrets and not the slightest softening of resolve through the winter and into spring. On a Tuesday morning in April 2002, four days before our darling's birthday, Jack took Hobbes to the vet for his monthly grooming. He was still able to walk then and do a few errands in his beloved Mercedes. They settled themselves in the waiting room. Someone started to struggle through the double doors to the vet's, and a woman emerged with a baby carrier in one hand and a pet carrier in the other. Setting down her loads, she asked the receptionist and the room at large, "Does anyone know the number of Pomeranian Rescue?"

The words were a gauntlet cast at Jack's feet. As soon as he had shoved Hobbes into the backseat of the car, he called me at work. "Now I'm not making any judgment," he began hastily, anticipating that my initial reaction would be 'no way in hell'. "Just let me tell you what happened."

As he recounted the meeting at the vet's, I thought, *No, no, no. This is terrible. No, this is too good to be true. Was it a bad break or serendipity?*

The coward was ostensibly leaving it up to me. Yet he had called, and the chance encounter felt like fate. I was impelled to jot down the phone number of the woman with the pet carrier and found myself already making an appointment for Wednesday.

Her white two-story wooden house was off a busy road, so I parked in the driveway. A tall, sturdy-looking woman in her thirties opened the door with a cheery blonde Pom at her feet.

"Don't you jump on Mrs. Davis, Scooby," she said to the dog in heel position at her side. "You'll ruin her hose."

The well-behaved young pooch showed no sign of jumping. He sat calmly and bounced his front paws a couple of times. As clearly as if he spoke out loud, he was saying, "I'm glad to see you. Play with me." Scooby had a face that could be used by Norman Rockwell. The caramel-colored eyes were bright and prominent, making him look pleasantly surprised and sharply alert. His good-sized ears stood up in attentive triangles, and his pink tongue was delicately extended a tad in eagerness to welcome me. He had to make the cutest canine portrait in Columbus, Ohio. In the whole county. The whole state.

"May I pick him up?" Cradled in my arms he was a nice load with thick fur and smelled of talcum powder. I felt his little heart beating and melted. "Scooby Doo?" I asked.

"Just Scooby."

"James Thurber said you should never bring the baby to the dog, always the dog to the baby."

She nodded awkwardly, probably pretending not to understand what I was talking about.

Scooby, calmly nestled in my arms, had already triggered love at first sight, but I set him back down and said I'd get back to her.

"Kismet," I told Jack the moment I got back home, and he agreed. It was meant to be.

When I went to pick up Scooby on Friday, Charlotte's birthday, the owner gave me the carrier, food bowls, a leash, a collar, plenty of food, his graduation certificate from obedience school and his AKC registration. "Be sure when he's groomed that they trim the fur around his foot pads," she said, "Because he *is* a Pomeranian."

Charlotte, lounging on the family-room couch, didn't move at first when I brought in the carrier and put it down next to her, but the golden retriever was immediately all nose. Scooby stepped out warily into his new home, wide-eyed and alone. He was a full-grown two-year-old Pom, but looked tiny compared to our golden retriever. Charlotte, easing herself up to a sitting position, began to stroke him and make him hers. We felt the pride of providing our daughter her dream gift, her dream dog.

It turned out that Pomeranians were my breed as well as Charlotte's. I loved Scooby's portability, enthusiasm and gallant look. Scooby's adoration of me, after Charlotte went off to Tufts University in Boston, was complete. I also liked the idea of having two dogs. Hobbes, the beautiful, gentle golden, had to be put down at 13, and we were down to one and utterly bereft.

Losing Scooby was impossible to contemplate. Poms live a long time compared to bigger dogs. Fifteen or so years is not uncommon. But in 2007 Scooby turned seven. He was getting up there. If I got an insurance dog soon, Jack and I would likely have canine company well into our seventies and not be called on to spend limited energy on raising a puppy. I wanted a puppy because older dogs can come with issues, and the animal shelter in Columbus had little selection of small dogs. Most of the shelter strays at the time were pit bulls or pit-bull mixes. Anyway, it was better to bond with a dog early and train him yourself, if you had the time and patience.

I searched the web for unwanted puppies and rescues. I haunted local dog shows. Eventually, giving up on finding another rescue, I wrote letters to Pom breeders listing my requirements "happy and healthy" and "show quality or close to it." I was not interested in the 'teacup' size, a trend that's incredibly cruel. The animals are fragile and usually suffer from a slew of health issues. Here we were taking highly sentient creatures, whose only desire is to please humans, and trying to mold them just so. We suppress some of their doggy nature for our convenience and encourage genetic traits and behaviors we like. Left to themselves all dogs would be mongrels, which after many generations would probably look like dingoes, according to Desmond Morris in his dictionary of dog breeds. Nonetheless, I snobbily wanted a purebred.

A breeder named Char in the town of Bark River in Michigan came back with good news. Char? Honest. Bark River? Honest. Char's Pomeranians had a litter with a male she thought would be a good fit for my family and ready to leave his home at 12 weeks old, or the middle of August 2008. She wanted a letter of recommendation from our vet. I was delighted. Some poor soul with love and a leash was not good enough for this puppy. You had to be vetted. The price would be $1,000. He was expensive and I imagined exquisite.

It was the stage when Jack could still drive, though with hand controls, and switch to the portable wheelchair at a destination. We agreed to meet Char at a Wendy's on the outskirts of Chicago, about halfway between her and us. Jack and I were finishing a burger and fries when a top-heavy, middle-aged woman in a hurry burst in looking for us. Leaving Jack in his portable wheelchair and carrying my large diet Coke, I followed her across the parking lot to a grassy verge set up with a portable fence enclosing several tiny animals.

"That's him," she said, pointing at a yellow ball of fuzz. The grass was only an inch-and-a-half high, but the tyke was so small he had to hop over it, endearing pushover me immediately. Looking at him from behind I could see a straight back, even hocks and tiny pointed ears seated just right on his head.

The breeder, scooping the puppy out of the pen, turned him so I could see his face. I locked eyes with the little guy, and that was it. He had sad eyes, almond-shaped and tilted down on the outer edges like a scholar looking up from translating a difficult tome, attempting to adjust to unexpected surroundings and a little worried. I knew I could soothe him.

I scanned his pedigree, suppressing a smile. "His grandmother's name is Looney Tune."

"And the dam is Tweety." She handed me the puppy and he began licking the back of my hand. His tail was so flat against the thick, downy puppy fur of his back that it fit like a puzzle piece.

I held my new treasure in my arms all the way home and called him Bertrand Russell. In his first few weeks, he came down with coccidia, a parasite that causes diarrhea. An un-housebroken dog with perpetual diarrhea meant perpetual cleaning up. I bought paper towels by the 24-pack and gallons of Nature's Miracle, a stain remover that promises to leave no scent. Russell slept in a crate next to my side of the bed, and Jack would wake me with a poke when he thought the puppy needed to go out.

"Russell is rustling," he'd say, and I would grab the rustler and sprint outside multiple times throughout the night. I was grateful my breed was not the Irish wolfhound.

"Russell is rustling," he said one night, poking me to make sure I heard.

"No, he's not," I said, and socked Jack in the ribs.

Needless to say, I couldn't get back to sleep. In bare feet I hauled the sick puppy down the stairs and out on the sharp late-summer grass. Russell recovered. He proved easy to train. He loved to fetch a ball. Scooby was the alpha dog, but Russell happily accommodated. They looked beautiful together, two golden boys trotting along, heads up, tails up in happy, prancing motion.

When Scooby eventually had to be put down, Jack and I agreed we didn't need another dog, nor more heartbreak or the job of raising another puppy. Then came the presidential election of 2016. Jack and I boarded a young man working on Hillary Clinton's campaign. He was never home, of course, working 16-hour days, and when he was, seemed to subsist on cherry tomatoes and coffee. On that horrific November Tuesday, we watched the returns from home, horrified at the midwestern states still shown in white on the map that needed to turn blue. They never did. Our boarder came in about 2 a.m. I greeted him on the stairs. His eyes were red and swollen. "This too shall pass," I told him with a wise maternal tone, the sort of thing Char would have said, and not what I really believed. He broke down in tears, disbelieving that a conman had taken over the country.

When morning came, it took a moment to understand why I felt like someone had died. It wasn't only that I thought Donald

Trump was a clown, a sociopathic narcissist and dangerously charismatic, not to mention an insult to my profession of public policy. I thought of Hillary as representing my gender, my generation's hopes and my college. She was two years behind me at Wellesley College, in the class of '69, and a political-science major. Hoo-hoo went to Wellesley, as did all her daughters. Even Mary, the daughter-in-law, was a Wellesley alumna, not to mention president of the class of 1950. I never met Hillary Rodham on campus, only at a couple of fundraisers later. While she was bringing Wellesley to terms with the Sixties, I was in the library researching my honors thesis, which used reams of data professing to show the *New York Times* was a tool of the federal government. One of my advisors told me it was the best thesis he'd ever seen in the department. Another thought it was about the worst. She was furious at my conceptual leaps. The truth was closer to her evaluation than his. I know at least one of my professors wrote a reference letter for both Hillary and me. I know which one he said could be president of the United States one day.

The loss was devastating to me, Jack and all my liberal compatriots. Little did I know then just how bad things would get. Distracted, I couldn't work at my desk. I could hardly pay attention to Jack. In my distress, I found myself at Char's Pomeranians website once again. And there he was, a brownish-blonde 12-week-old lying on his tummy, back feet splayed out, with a red ball between his feet. He looked up eagerly towards someone out of the picture, as if begging for a home.

A month after the disaster of an election, Ari's arrival turned out to be the salve I needed. Jack was not enthusiastic but bowed to the inevitable. Steve was delighted. He played ball with the puppy, making him sit and then counting *one, two, three... three and a half* extremely slowly before tossing it from the couch in my loft office all the way through the long bathroom and to the far wall of the bedroom. Squeaking the ball madly, the puppy would return to Steve for a reprise.

After the ritual mutual sniffing and a few weeks to settle in, Ari recognized he would have to train his companion Pom, who was only just emerging from Scooby's shadow and recovering from his lifelong domination.

"I'm the only dog here," he had begun to realize in his dim-witted way with great relief. He was pleasantly settling into a life where he was allowed to make a decision, such as to eat his kibble. Ari took care of that. Russell was not allowed to eat until Ari was done. And, unfortunately, food was Russell's main reason to live. Ari expected service, so I sat cross-legged on the tile kitchen floor, placing a few pieces at a time of his regionally sourced organic kibble on my knee so he could put up his front paws and savor the morning repast. With my right hand I petted the silent, super-fuzzy Russell. If I offered him food, he shook his head and turned away. When Ari was sated, Russell gingerly approached his bowl. Ari sniffed it to make sure he didn't need one more morsel. Then he allowed his foot soldier a turn.

I escorted both Ari and Russell for us to be trained in obedience. Russell was a star at the Columbus All-Breed Training Center doggy school, brilliant at heeling, able to sit and stay in a row of dogs, all much larger than him, even while I left the room with the other handlers for five timed minutes. I would return to find my dog looking worried, but perfectly in line, even though another had broken.

Ari was a gifted heeler, too. At seven months, he could heel fast or slowly, do about-turns and figure-eights. Generals must know the correct way to march so they can sit on a hill and judge the troops as they slog through the muck below. Ari was just shy of show material, toy royalty. Heeling smartly in the ring was in his genes. Other simple commands passed over his little head. In puppy obedience class, the trainer, for fun, had us take turns hiding while our dogs were distracted. We then called out our dog's name. Every dog but Ari searched eagerly for his or her pet parent. I kneeled behind a plastic block on the other side of the ring, nose in communication with the beery flooring, and shouted Ari and bellowed his full name, Aristotle, but he willfully ignored me. Clearly I was the one who was supposed to come when called.

7

THE MERITS OF BREATHING

A chaplain popped in as I lay drowsily on the hospital bed during my third chemo treatment. I assumed she was some version of Christian. But it turned out she wasn't there to pardon my sins, which I was certain wouldn't do me much good anyway. She was a Buddhist offering spiritual support.

"I just read a *New Yorker* article about Buddhism," I said, struggling to enunciate from the soft mattress through a Benadryl fog. "They reviewed a book that says Buddhism is practical. Meditation as self-help."

She only nodded. She was there to empathize, not proselytize. She asked about my support system, and I told her I'd been willing to ask for help and overwhelmed by the flood of kindness. She said it was good I was able to ask.

I wanted to talk more about Buddhism, which always had a mystical sheen about it, but my words were slurring. "I'm sorry, I've got a sedative running through me and it's making it hard to think."

Perhaps it was an omen, a clue from the universe. I'd been reading about Buddhism and a practitioner unexpectedly showed up at my bedside. My clouded mind flashed *maybe I should look into becoming a Buddhist.*

The teachings of Buddhism seemed heart-centered and compassionate, and I thought a little spirituality could only help my recovery. Later, back at home, I reread the *New Yorker* piece by Adam Gopnik reviewing *Why Buddhism Is True*. The author, Robert Wright, claimed Buddhism recognizes that the central fact of life is loss, most notably death. We can reduce suffering by sitting still and simply breathing. He skips the supernatural aspects of the religion, the fundamental one being the notion of reincarnation.

I broke away from my task-ridden desk and joined Aristotle on the cozy red couch in my loft office, where he was happily curled up, dozing. Russell was downstairs guarding the house, ready for existential threats. The ultimate menace was the overfed, overlong, steel-gray tomcat that hunted the garden for birds and families of mice. He frequently crossed our wooden deck, tauntingly past the sliding doors to the family room. If the cat poured into sight, slinking like a leopard on silent paws, I knew it would send Russell into a paroxysm of barking. If Ari were on guard downstairs as well, he would levitate, with all four paws up off the ground at once.

As I settled on the sofa beside him, Ari unwound drowsily for a petting session. Lying on his back, he trusted his belly to my gentle hand. The skin was smooth as velvet. He elevated one haunch and patiently waited for my fingers to attend to something that prickled. He turned to look into my eyes. The retinas were deep black and the irises a chocolaty brown with a thin black rim I'd never noticed. Even the whites were tinged a milky brown. Short white fur with a few black whiskers fanned from his shiny black nose. I was surprised at how they radiated away from the quotations of his nostrils.

"Have you given any thought to metaphysics?" I asked my drowsing furry blonde boy. "Ethics?"

Still stroking his velvety ears and fur, I glanced at my bookcase. There was a shelf of dog books, one called *Inside of a Dog*. It starts with a joke. "Ari, did you know that 'outside of a dog, a book is a man's best friend'?" I paused for a comic effect. "Inside of a dog, it's too dark to read... Marx said that," I explained, "Groucho Marx."

Ari extended his tongue in a yawn. It was multiple shades of pink and lavender, the top a bit rough, and the bottom wet and shiny and vulnerable. Poms have a double coat two inches deep and as warm and luxurious as a sultry summer evening. I burrowed my fingers down to the smooth skin on his back, and he was wakefully still.

We were both happy. That's why Buddha looks happy, I suppose. He's been petting his dog.

Buddhists believe that as part of the *samsara* life and death cycle we can come back as cats, goldfish, black-masked Tanganyikan lovebirds, elephants, cockroaches and, hey, dogs. From a Buddhist perspective, all animals and sentient beings were equally precious and fellow journeyers on the path to enlightenment. In turn, animals can be reincarnated as humans. If all that were true, I would prefer to return to earth as a Yeatsian bird "of hammered gold and gold enameling to set upon a golden bough" singing my precious metal heart out. Reincarnation was a far-out extension of another Buddhist belief, the interconnectedness of all life. The latter was easy for this westerner to latch onto, possibly for lack of effort, and not as chubby a target for humor.

Pantheism was part of our own literature. It was embedded in my weeks and months in the White Mountains of New Hampshire, the deserts of Southern California, the savannas of Africa and travels over a lifetime. It was embedded in the peaceful green surroundings of our home and Windrush Pond that lay beyond our deep backyard, our own little Walden Pond, with a tall, high-spewing fountain. Russell once walked himself around it, when I was too lazy for anything long and had let him out the back door to the deck instead. Terrified a coyote had abducted him, I anxiously combed the neighborhood. Then he appeared in the distance, clearly completing our standard circumnavigation, head up and cheerily prancing.

The pond had attracted generations of great blue herons, green herons, mallards and Canada geese. It was Jack who had stocked the pond with large-mouth bass and bluegills when he was president of the community association, as well as white amurs, algae-eating carp. The carp grew to a couple feet long and sometimes thrashed up to the surface, making a Midwest version of Big Sur. Windrush felt like countryside, or as close as we could come to it, with the corollary benefits to the spirit. I remembered reading Thoreau in tenth grade.

He knew how to break from the hurly burly, seeking out serenity and solitude in nature.

"How am I connected to you?" I asked Aristotle as we sat on my comfortable couch in my sturdy house in my small community trying hard to be green and neighborly. By touch, pleasure and our stillness. At least for the moment, I was living Buddhist precepts of patience, trust and acceptance.

I didn't think about it when the Buddhist chaplain visited, and the drugs in my system were attacking those triple-negative invaders, but what I was still successfully blocking out was the essence of Buddhism, an internalization of the inexorable, inevitable reality of suffering.

Not that I lacked respect for illness and suffering. There was Jack, after all. And Russell and I had done our share of hospital visits. He was so good at heeling, I thought he'd shine at healing. He passed the tests to become a certified therapy dog. For six years we motored once a week to a nearby hospital to minister to patients. We were assigned a regular floor, and after making ourselves known to the nurses and other staff, who enjoyed the visits as much as the patients did, would make rounds. Russell lay on a patient's bed to be petted, communicating love and forgiveness while secretly hoping that would earn him a treat. The world was a little much for him unless Swiss cheese was involved.

Not everybody we ran into was thrilled at the idea. I once knocked cheerily on a door and opened it to find a large Somali family. Standing in the doorway, with the Pom sitting in a correct heeling position by my left leg, I asked, "Would you like a visit from a therapy dog?"

They all stared at me silently as if I were peddling moonshine.

"Sorry." We backed out.

They say that dogs understand illness and sadness, and know they are providing comfort. I'm not sure that Russell was into it. His presence was an icebreaker for conversation, though, most often of the social kind, giving ill people a bit of respite from the sadness and bleakness of usual hospital life. Sometimes it got serious.

"I'm terminal," an older gent shared with me, an admission I wasn't prepared for. With a deep suntan, he didn't look especially ill.

His hands, stroking Russell, were large and weathered. I imagined he was a farmer, or at least worked with his hands.

"I'm sorry," I said, and luckily the patient turned to how he would be going home to his daughter's house. I was relieved to know that he had a daughter and thought of my own father, who lost the battle, too.

Ari was my own uncertified therapy dog. Being with him could be meditative, though whenever an airplane passed overhead, visible from the window behind us and making a noise that he could hear, he would leap to the top of the back of the sofa to try to catch it.

Meditation is therapeutic, Robert Wright wrote in *Why Buddhism Is True*, and as such very American. It was certainly popular. They offered a meditation course at the New Albany club. Concentrate on your breathing. Take a slow breath in and a slow breath out. Repeat. You're not going anywhere. You aren't waiting for something to happen, good or bad. Whatever you do, get rid of random thoughts: tame your 'monkey mind'. Stop the compulsive running around and live in the moment. In rigorous studies, scientists have found support for the hypothesis that meditation reduces pain, both physical and emotional. It was worth a try, and I decided to put it way up in the B section of my to-do lists to follow up, using a location where Ari wouldn't come looking for me.

Maybe the A-list. I thought of the Norse story about life being like a bird that flies into a lighted hall out of darkness, then out the other end into darkness, the story where 'live' is task two.

What were the sub-tasks for flying through the light? Do as many loop-a-whirls as you could get in? How does one skirt the devastating anxiety, brooding and sorrow that go with the inevitability of task three while you're hacking your way through task two? Surely the answer is not to fly as fast as you can. Nor to feel like you're in a perpetual waiting room.

8

IN THE SWING AGAIN

Fall had passed in a blink since my cancer diagnosis that summer of 2017. The holiday season was jingling its way in, and, luckily, I was recovering well from my third chemo treatment. I only had one more to go when Jack and I arrived at Josh and Lorraine's house for Thanksgiving dinner. We contributed roasted Brussels sprouts with pecans, a couple of bottles of wine and our traditional family dessert of ice-cream turkeys. A scoop of vanilla ice cream covered in chocolate sat on a fan-shaped cookie that looked just a bit like a turkey tail. Red, yellow and orange icing made the eyes, beak and wavy wattles.

The living room was denuded of Legos, race tracks, stuffed animals and action figures. The scent of roasting turkey and garlicky potatoes filled the house. Lorraine also made a tofurkey, since she and her family were vegetarians. Lorraine's mother and aunts arrived with several more aromatic dishes. Her mother's family is French, for which I was eternally grateful, particularly at mealtime.

Josh and Lorraine met with a reluctant kiss precisely at midnight. The first Jack and I knew of her was one evening, over a year later, when Josh finished up dinner at our house and said he had to leave to pick up creamed spinach for a sick friend. This was extremely odd. Josh would never willingly eat creamed spinach

75

himself. We held our tongues. "She's vegetarian," he added. On the last day of the year 2000, a group of college friends had gotten together for a New Year's Eve party in Columbus. As the ball dropped in Times Square, a mutual friend said everybody had to find a person to kiss and paired painfully shy Josh and slightly-less-shy Lorraine. They didn't see each other again for another year, when Lorraine's laptop crashed. She remembered Josh was a geek and tracked him down. The laptop continued to be fractious, and Josh had to make several trips, stayed longer and longer to talk, and their relationship blossomed.

Before meeting Lorraine, Josh had dated some interesting girls. When he was at Kenyon College, he told us how a classmate took him to meet her parents in a high-rise Chicago building overlooking Lake Michigan.

"Right on the lake?" asked Jack, impressed. The location was as ritzy as it gets.

"Who's the girl?" I asked.

"Her mother's maiden name is…" he said, dropping an eponymous word for wealth.

"Tell us about her," said Jack, hoping for super girl.

"Well, she's fine when she's on her lithium."

Thank goodness for Lorraine and her solid Norman roots. Her family knows the important stuff, not frou-frou cuisine, but real food à la française. Donnie and Lisal made their way through the door balancing a huge tray of hors d'oeuvres and a coconut cream pie. Donnie opened the wine we had brought, the white a Chablis and the red a 2002 Château Gloria. He scrutinized the Bordeaux, pulled out his phone and tapped out something. "I'm checking Vivino," he said and then added, "This bottle is worth $545." Jack had bought it for less than $50 some 10 years earlier.

Unfortunately, the wine tasted like 2017 Docetaxel and Cyclophosphamide. I took two sips and gave up. The food wasn't much better. My pleasure came from sitting next to Vincent.

He glanced up at me with his big dark eyes and asked, "When do we get the ice-cream turkeys?"

"First you eat your dinner."

He tried to make a deal with me on how much turkey and other stuff on his plate he had to eat before he could have dessert. We settled on five bites of turkey.

"You know your great-grandmother's uncle changed the date of Thanksgiving," I told him. This was not going to impress a four-year-old. In a few years, I would tell him the full story, if I made it until then. It was a true story. Uncle Fred's achievement was even a question on *Jeopardy!* under the category of holidays. I may not be phrasing the answer exactly right but it was something like: "Fred Lazarus persuaded President Roosevelt to change the date of this holiday feast."

Again I veered to another topic, hoping to take Vincent's mind off dessert. "What do you want Santa Claus to bring you for Christmas?"

"Maybe an ice-cream turkey," he said mournfully.

Walking into the hospital for the fourth round of chemo, knowing it would be my last, I felt hugely relieved, joyful even. At home that evening, I was too sick to lift myself off the family-room couch or pet the occasional blonde dog that padded by. Buried beneath blankets up to my chin, I watched old *Midsomer Murders* episodes and couldn't add up the number of murders. Every cell in my body was engaged in mortal combat.

It was early December, and with chemo behind me, my body would be allowed to heal. Time's golf cart was back there, but its dust wasn't bringing tears to my eyes. My hair was starting to grow in, fresh and velvety, and it looked like it would be curly. Curly hair, when mine had always been straight except for the cowlicks, was a gift. Also, there was no more need for extra help. I could pretend life was back to normal.

Normal at our house at holiday time was madness. I Santa-tized the family room. That is, Steve brought the tree, three boxes of ornaments and various pillows and tchotchkes up from the basement, then did most of the work. At first I pointed from the sofa regally to where stuff should go. In a few days, I was able to do my own decorating. Cheerful cards poured in, and I carefully arranged them on the mantel, the bar and every available surface in the family room. UPS and FedEx drivers stuffed cardboard boxes through the door continually and sprinted for their trucks so they could speed on. We maneuvered them into the living room with the artificial tree cluttered with eccentric but meaningful ornaments from 40-odd years of collecting. Charlotte would have preferred a minimalist design statement, all silver trim perhaps. Ours was beyond eclectic. Back when we cut a live Christmas tree, for several years we invited Jewish friends over for a tree-trimming party. Jack assured them that untangling tree lights was an important Christian ritual and they were such good friends we would let them in on it.

By the Friday before Christmas our living room was uninhabitable, but the wheelchair and I could fit in the family room as usual for a cozy dinner for two. I lit candles that filled the air with holiday scents: the likes of fir, cranberries, cinnamon and cloves. I lit a match in the fireplace to dry wood that quickly caught and warmed and brightened the room. I carefully placed an arrangement of pine branches in a vase on the coffee table. The room smelled of pine, wood smoke and spices. I set Jack's hospital tray and my TV tray with the Marimekko placemats we bought when the kids were little. The bright blue backgrounds and big white snowflakes sang Christmas cheer. The Volkswagen Beetle with a Christmas tree lying on the roof was my favorite. I dug down in a drawer for red napkins. All was bright.

I trimmed green beans to steam and added kosher salt. I roasted new potatoes in olive oil, then broiled a pair of gleaming tuna steaks, adding a sprinkling of dill. The fat and calories would follow as a selection from a cornucopia of Christmas cookies.

I cut up Jack's tuna for him. He took a bite and was seized with a coughing fit. A peach-colored Fiesta-ware bowl that clashed with the décor was the first to come to hand. Jack spat the bubbly white phlegm into it over and over.

I punched in 911 and didn't ask them not to use the sirens, as usual, to avoid unnecessarily disturbing the neighbors. Jack coughed and expelled. Death by grilled tuna fish? The wild warning sounds drew closer and louder and more alarming, then abruptly stopped.

Three imposing, reassuring men from the fire department busted into our holiday tableau in their black uniforms, clanking with equipment. Jack was still spitting. They took his pulse, blood pressure and oxygen level and asked him if he needed to go to the hospital. The coughing was about over, and, no, Jack did not want to go to the hospital. The EMTs said to call them anytime it happened again. After the routine callouts when, despite Steve's or my efforts, Jack fell, I usually baked banana bread and ferried it over, still-warm and sweet-scented from the oven, as a thank-you. I figured I'd bring them banana bread made with candied fruit for a change.

In the surprising new calm, Jack turned on a murder mystery. I'd wanted to see *Love Actually,* a light-hearted holiday rom-com. It was my favorite and an annual tradition, as if I needed more tradition. Jack wasn't into romance, though, and I figured under the circumstances it was his choice. The remote was something Jack could still control.

I readied my patient for bed, brushing his teeth and taking off his shoes and compression socks. I undressed him and handed him his pills and helped him sip water in between. Two different antidepressants, a med for bladder control and one to prevent his limbs from spasming.

Jack said nothing about the visit from the goon squad. In the warm yellow glow of the bedside lamp, he turned on his iPad and dove into an audiobook. He was in an Anthony Trollope phase, absorbing everything the man wrote, which was close to infinite. I adjusted his headphones and watched him settle in.

I didn't want to jar Jack with schmaltz, so I kept quiet. Pity and sorrow coursed through my heart at his endless equanimity. I leaned over and kissed him on the forehead. He knew what I meant. With the dogs snuggled at the foot of the bed headed towards sleep, I lay down myself, but my mind whirred with random thoughts, ratcheting up my anxiety.

MS robs all muscles of nerve signals. It must be affecting throat muscles, the ones that swallow. We never got to the Christmas cookies. Springerle, sweet and airy. Gingery, hard Pfeffernüsse. Maybe I can catch Love Actually *tomorrow night. Hugh Grant. Mmmm, cute cookie. Softer food? Would I have to feed him? What exactly was going to get him? How soon? If I die before him, will he be okay?*

I scrambled desperately, aware of the shattered dome that used to be the sky, the black pit above it and the stars streaming away into pin pricks and nothingness.

Was life with Jack becoming dedicated to evading the truth? Doctors always seem to have something more they can do. I would call the neurologist first thing in the morning.

After the last infusion of body-slamming beneficial chemicals, early in December as the holidays approached, I began exercising. The Spielman Center naturally had a gym, a breezy, white-painted room packed with equipment like a treadmill, weights and balance balls, and a fine view out a picture window. It was a safe place to get going again if you lacked breasts on your chest and hair on your head. The physical therapist had me stretch the ipsilateral arm up a wall trying to reach 90 degrees, then the contralateral arm. At home I practiced, and soon could raise both arms. I lifted two-pound weights, then three, then five.

Tennis was over, however. Enough of losing on the New Albany gold team. When the last ball goes out of bounds, follow it. "Are you sure?" Jack asked after I told him I was hanging up my racket. "Won't you miss it?" He was in his electric wheelchair, the seatbelt tight to keep him from sliding forward and buffered metal wings pressing each side of his chest to hold him upright.

On Christmas morning, we traditionally opened presents from the immediate family and then, bearing gifts, toddled over to Donnie and Lisal's in the evening for a feast with the extended fam and selected friends. Lisal decorated her house like a mall, with a large tree on each of three levels of their rambling, farmhouse-style home, a vast collection of 18-inch-high nutcrackers and blazing red candles galore. Fifteen or so merry bodies, spanning three generations, crowded into the upstairs living area. Jack had no place to move in the melee, and I tried to stick with him as much as I could. He felt helpless and alone in the crowd and would get visibly grumpy if I deserted him for long. Not that he said anything.

It wasn't easy to keep vigil by Jack's chair, what with making my way to the Sauvignon and the Cabernet down one floor and finding a relative I hadn't seen in ages, then back up only to encounter someone else on the stairs. I resented having to hover over my husband, and was relieved when Babette or someone else made the effort to lean down and talk to him.

The appetizer, Lisal's inimitable cheese fondue, graced the coffee table. We stuck pieces of bread onto skewers, helping the young'uns spin sweet, tangy melted cheese without drips. Lisal called for the present opening to begin. Dinner would follow. Kids headed to the pile by the tree and plunged in, grabbing shiny boxes and bags and strewing wrapping paper with abandon. The oldest generation, mine, and 'the kids', in their thirties and forties, were assigned to each other in a gift exchange. The grandchildren bagged loot from everybody. In the densely furnished living room, the adults bumped past each other to find the packages with our names. My giver was Donnie.

One great Christmas pleasure was oddly shaped packages. Donnie's gift to me looked like a bottle of wine, but was a little too short and too cylindrical. I ripped open the wrapping paper to find a can of tennis balls with a handwritten note: *Get yourself a new racket at the club.* I'd forgotten that a couple of years earlier I put a tennis racket on my Amazon wish-list. I'd never taken it off.

"That's too big a gift," I protested.

"Nope," he insisted, "it isn't."

I shook the can, and it made that satisfying thumping that promised good times. I felt a glint of optimism. I showed the can and message to Jack, perched beside me. He looked at me, smiling, his eyes shimmering through the ground-glass, semi-opacity of his glasses. "Do it."

Maybe one more season. Tennis, like gambling, is a rush, irresistible and addictive. The most stubborn or foolish of our breed persist into old age.

So I signed up for my usual team at the country club. I went to the gym religiously all winter. And I walked, getting up to three miles, according to the Fitbit.

When spring came, I dressed for Monday morning practices as if donning a suit of armor. My pair of triangular rubbery prostheses slid into slots in a bra specially made for a woman who doesn't have her own bosom. It was heavy on my blank chest. A white top with red trim in the latest no-iron, flexible fabric covered the bra. I pulled on a white skort, the shorts tight on my thighs and buttocks. I donned a New Albany baseball cap and new prescription sunglasses framed in bright blue, then cute socks and fancy new kicks.

9

LIVE FOR IT

My body still felt torn apart, but I'd made it through cancer treatment and wanted my life back. Jack was holding his own as best he could. Looming, if I let it, was the prospect of a malign invasion of another organ. My most reliable escape was tennis. It steadied and focused my mind. It whisked away tension and stress, and put me in a good mood, especially when I won. Jack said it made me easier to get along with. Donnie's gift of a new racket was an expression of hope. Through the winter and spring of 2018 I fought to gain back strength and agility, with the help of long walks under the clouds of winter that at their worst spewed rain and sleet and at best snowflakes that took over from the grayness. Columbus is the cloudiest city in America after Seattle, and the latter has an ocean and mountains to compensate. Twice weekly I visited a personal trainer at New Albany, who worked me hard, always ending with a special stretch for my chest muscles. You lock your hands behind you and pull back and feel a satisfying expansion. My pecs were all there, thankfully, but often tightened painfully because of the surgery. I would have to watch out to keep the silicone frauds in place. I worried they would slip down, or worse, one would slip down and I'd have a bizarrely crooked chest.

It would be my eighth year on the ladies' gold team at the New Albany club in the eastside suburbs of Columbus. Women were called 'ladies', but men 'men' rather than 'gentlemen'. 'Gold' was a euphemism for 'old,' meaning fifty and older. Club teams ordinarily field five courts, with court five the lowest, the least competitive match, the one the player on her last legs was assigned. I was about as old as you could go and as low as you could get. The practices and the matches would open up escape several hours a week, away from the weary routine of cheering Jack, nursing him and anticipating his needs. Away from worrying about newly growing peanuts.

After finishing Wednesday morning practice in June, Judy, our team captain, told me, "You and Louise will be on court five tomorrow."

I didn't know Louise, but the bottom court of our doubles team was familiar clay. After Columbus Country Club, we would play a dozen matches over a couple of months, some of them at home and some in the far reaches of the suburbs.

A teammate sidled up to whisper into my left hearing aid. It was full of sweat but still working. "You'll have to keep score for Louise."

I couldn't hear and she couldn't count. I was used to shaky, fraying and fragile partners. One had suffered a chronically painful foot and couldn't plant it properly to return a ball. Another was younger and fitter but had one stroke, a forehand slice. If that was your only forehand, the other team would catch on, play up close and shoot you in the ankles. I tried to avoid playing with the woman. Then she died. Pancreatic cancer. Now I felt for her, missed her and kept imagining I would see her yellow VW at the club. One year I was paired with a woman with a neck brace. She walked like a stork, everything following the neck. She couldn't bend down. We lost every match, one crushing defeat after another, lucky even to squeeze out a few games.

I liked to tell people I am five-feet tall, but the best I had ever measured was a quarter inch shy of that. At 72, I was probably shrinking. A lob over my head that landed two feet in the court was my bitter enemy. My forehand likes to take a long weekend in Chicago and the serve a beach vacation in Jamaica. There was the deafness, but I wasn't quite as deaf as the poles that held up a tennis net, and much of the game could be communicated with the hands.

Satisfaction was meeting a yellow ball with a solid thrum of drum-tight strings in the sweet middle of the racket. There is no other sound like it, a beautiful sound that sets the heart singing. Sometimes I even won. Hope flew up unbidden like the optimistic skyward toss of a serve.

A breeze from the open sunroof soothed the anxiety as I wound through the long, leisurely entrance to the Columbus Country Club in my newly washed red BMW the next morning, admiring the old-growth trees and taking in the scent of shorn summer grass. I had no trouble finding the tennis courts. I'd lost on them before. The fence behind one court flaunted banners from previous gold team league championships. Five of them over the previous six years. My chest felt tight in the muscles that had surrounded my breasts. My mastectomy bra with squishy inserts was a dead weight under my team tee. My brand-new racket was neatly stowed in the backseat in a cheery Vera Bradley case patterned in rows of elephants.

I joined my teammates. One slipped over and said in my ear as quietly as she could for me to be able to hear, "Keep score for Louise. She can't." I was getting the message.

The Columbus Country Club captain and ours alternated calling out the court assignments. As we turned to the battlefield, one more teammate tapped me on the shoulder. "You'll have to keep the score. And tell her where to go." She meant I would have to make sure Louise was on the correct side of the court, ad or deuce, and whether she was receiving or at the net.

I didn't have a great memory myself and couldn't remember names. It was a lifelong problem, not a new one, though dementia was one of my worries, as it probably was for most people in my age group who can remember to worry. I kept tabs on the score when it was my serve, but otherwise went with what was agreed on.

I figured if we lost quickly we could get to the snacks before the other courts. Our opponents' club had superb two-bite cinnamon rolls, sweet, tangy and not sinful if you've exercised. Maybe there would be chicken salad too.

Louise and I looked at each other. She was medium height with the grandmotherly build of a healthy older woman.

"We're here to have fun and do our best," I told her.

She agreed with a wrinkly, cheerful smile.

"Forehand or backhand?" I asked.

"I play forehand."

The other team clanked open the gate to court five. One of them had two knee braces and the other a single one. Limits to mobility were not only a good sign for our chances on the court, but ready mnemonics.

"Hi, I'm Ellen," said the first one. "We haven't seen each other for a long time."

I knew her mother-in-law well. How was Ellen old enough to be in this league? The other was Jane, and thank goodness she didn't tell me how well we knew each other.

We warmed up on the newly rolled clay. It would be easy to tell if a ball was in or out, at least for the first set. It would leave a definitive mark. I savored the giving surface through my K-Swiss kicks, branded '7.0', the highest level in tennis. Real tennis shoes for serious players, people who knew how to use the clay surface. I imagined sliding my lead foot in at 45 degrees and blocking a ball into a doubles alley with my stick. The pros called their rackets sticks. I had a new stick, and relished its firm grip.

As I feared, our opponents stroked the ball with the assurance of women who had taken lessons since they started coming to the country club at the age of three, and their mothers needed something for them to do besides swimming. We warmed up with mini tennis, groundstrokes and net play. An opponent's feed to me hit the net and drifted a foot or two beyond where I could reach it with my racket.

"Come," I told the ball. "They never come when they're called," I said to One-Brace as she fetched it.

We practiced serves. Ellen Two-Braces' was hard, direct and had topspin. All I would be able to do was return the ball in the direction it came, hopefully at the same speed. Jane One-Brace's serve was softer. Might offer an opening.

"Margarita or martini?" One-Brace asked as she prepared to spin for serve. The butt of her racket was not a mere 'up' or 'down' but sported a cute sticker.

"Margarita," said Louise.

My partner proved to be a good tennis player. Yes, I had to move her aside once when she wandered to the baseline thinking it was her serve when it was mine. Yes, she looked like she felt sore, her left hip leaning out a bit. Oddly, she frequently positioned herself a little behind the service line in no man's land. Still more oddly, the balls came to her. One would arrive like a homing pigeon at the center of her racket strings, and she would direct it with an effortless, though unrecommended arm-only swing at an impossible-to-return slant or overhead into a corner beyond gimpy Two-Brace and One-Brace.

We rallied vigorously and went to deuce a couple of times but lost the first set 6-2. The goal to have fun was being met. I held in check my bloodlust for a win. A cardinal sang cheer, cheer, cheer, high in a tall oak. The azure sky beckoned as I started the second set, sending the ball up skyward for a meek but accurate thwack. The serve had opted not to take flight for that vacation in Jamaica.

I wondered whether the club would provide both iced tea and lemonade and, if so, whether I should combine them in an Arnold Palmer.

One-Brace's serve consistently went short to my backhand. Several times in the first set, I hit it back too hard and sharply. Out. Worse, those were unforced errors. A steady serve and return of serve are the two things you must have in tennis. I needed to touch One-Brace's serve softly and safely. I focused on the mid-point of the right side of the opponent's service box. One-Brace's ball came in far to my left, exactly where I wanted it. I hit a deft, gentle backhand drop shot. One-Brace raced gimpily to the ball, leaning in as it hit the clay and lay down for a dust bath.

"Love 40," One-Brace called out loud and clear as I prepared to receive.

My bet was that, put off by my sudden ability to return the backhand, One-Brace would serve to my forehand. She did, and I returned it deep to her backhand corner. Her return was bound to be defensive. Louise and I anticipated a soft lob, which Louise, from her ball-beckoning position behind the service line, socked down the middle in the narrow opening among the three braces and one healthy knee. The opponents' lips formed moues of disappointment. They weren't thinking *yours*. The ball wasn't anybody's. Game.

Two-Brace looked confused. "Do we switch?"

"What?" I said, probably too loud, one of the common sins of the deaf.

One-Brace looked even more perplexed. "Who just served?"

Two-Brace stared at us in blank-eyed confusion. "Have we played two games on that side?"

We all went silent. Then Louise said authoritatively to Two-Brace, "We switch and it's your serve."

I looked at the game score. We were ahead 4-3. We could win the set. But if we won, we would have to go to a third, postponing the cinnamon rolls. And the Arnold Palmer. Was that worth throwing the game? Never. Two-Braces would serve next and probably win. Then it would be Louise's turn, my fuzzy-headed but dependable partner. We could do it. I positioned my 7.0 feet just behind the white tape at the baseline on the deuce side. I bounced the ball twice, watching it create shallow shadows in the soft clay.

I stood up straight and sent the yellow ball vertically into the unshatterable dome of sky, living for it.

10

MY FATHER'S FAULT

Tennis is a lifetime sport, my father told me about the time I was able to walk a few city blocks with him on Lexington Avenue, holding his hand while we headed downtown to the Doubleday bookshop. When opportunity struck, he set me on the road to a lifetime with a racket.

Richard Witkind, my dad, was the handsomest man in New York. I can say that because his brother Lloyd, who haunted the city's café society in the Fifties, dating actresses and models, was named the second handsomest man in New York in a column of a major newspaper, the *Post* maybe. They were both the classic tall, dark type. The story may well be apocryphal, but I knew who the best-looking man in the city was.

My parents divorced when I was about two, and it was just me and my birth mother in a tiny apartment in Hempstead, Long Island. That's when she went mad. I didn't know who Gladys was screaming at or why she was crying and in pain. Whenever she was raging helplessly, I hid under a table holding tight to the cat. He didn't tend to stay long, slipping out of my arms in a puff of silky oyster-gray fur as soon as he got a chance. After the real grown-ups, my father and paternal grandmother, figured out what was going on, they sent Gladys away and I moved in with the latter.

"Mommy had to go to a rest home," the adults told me. When Gladys didn't have to rest anymore and was released from the home, she escaped to Florida. It wasn't far enough. She headed overseas to Dublin. From there she landed in St. Patrick's Hospital, a mental asylum established by Jonathan Swift, and lived out her life there, heavily medicated, dying in 1982.

When my grandmother took me in as a pre-school child, all I understood was that my mother had left me. Only when I was a bit older did she provide an explanation that was, if anything, less credible than a need for a spa vacation. Gladys thought the president of US Steel was trying to kill her with rays from his television tower. That was the short story; I never dug up a longer one. No place was safe from the incessant pain of rays, whatever that meant, focused on her brain. All that was left of Gladys were a few teddy bears she'd carefully named Henry, Herbert and Anatole. In my mid-seventies, I still kept them in a drawer.

My dad found a woman friend. I never met her but knew she was Chinese and worked for the Library of Congress. He took the train to Washington to spend weekends with her. After that, he dated quite seriously a French woman who worked for her delegation at the United Nations. I liked her okay. She gave me beautiful dolls in traditional costume from Brittany, Aquitaine and other French regions. What was not to like? Then she was posted to Algeria, and I don't believe my father ever contacted her again.

I was rescued when my dad married Char. Like her mother before her, Charlotte Lazarus Gorman was a strong, liberated woman before the women's liberation movement of the Sixties kicked off. She had three children from her first marriage and a full-time volunteer day job as vice president of the New York City League of Women Voters. Char was not going to settle for anything less than a binding commitment. Her first husband, Warren Gorman, was a psychiatrist, and from long tutorials with him she decided she'd learned enough that she was one, too. That was close to the truth. From the start, Char nurtured me, talked to me, listened, and showed me what it would be like to be a grown woman.

Char and the kids lived in a 12th-floor apartment on East 96th Street. She was originally from Columbus, Ohio, a place somewhere in the west. I was one of those city kids who had never heard of Schenectady, and hardly even knew about Albany, the state capital. It was all 'upstate', a mysterious wilderness. And west was anywhere beyond the Hudson River.

Char added Witkind to her name when I was 12 in 1958. I dug my heels in and refused to leave my grandmother's quiet, spacious-for-two apartment, along a leafy street of brownstones that was used as the exterior location for Holly Golightly and her ginger cat's home in *Breakfast's at Tiffany's*. After a period of resistance, I joined five other people in a smaller apartment. There was 14-year-old Bobby, two years older than me; Babette, seven years younger; and Donnie, born in 1947, only 18 months younger. All of them called their mom Char. So did everybody else. I started calling my dad Dick, like the others.

Babette was only five and adjusted to having an extra sibling with aplomb. She was dark-eyed and dainty, with an outsized vocabulary and the beginnings of a gorgeous singing voice. Tiny for her age, she was too short to press the '12' on the building's elevator, so coming home she would press eight and use the stairs for the last four floors. Babette was born mellow. Our Jamaican cook in New York summed it up: "She's been here before." She meant the little girl had the calmness and wisdom of someone familiar with the planet from birth. As it turned out, unlike me, Babette did not especially like to study. When she somehow landed on the Dean's List at Berkeley, she framed the certificate and gave it to Dick because she knew he would like it. She didn't especially care. I've always admired Babette's easy calm, her sense of humor and ability to go with the flow. Though Bobby was perpetually reserved, he introduced me to his collection of sci-fi books and let me watch him practice jazz piano. Even as a teen, he dressed like he had money. Donnie, outgoing and quick to smile, was casual before it was cool. To get home, they both frequently had to walk at different times by a dark, full-block armory along a long crosstown street. Bobby was robbed there more than once by people who spotted him as likely to have a few bucks. Donnie was never approached.

For a long time Donnie and I were close to the same height. He was athletic, though that included routinely breaking his glasses in games of basketball at school. We developed love and respect for each other and, naturally, fervent rivalries. He preferred the Peanuts comic; I, Pogo. If merchandise sales were a marker, he won over time. Peanuts comics and Snoopy dolls were still around. You had to trawl through eBay to find memorabilia of the worldly wise Pogo Possum and his pal Albert the alligator.

Donnie and I enjoyed being at odds. He claimed Michelangelo the better artist; I, Leonardo da Vinci. We'd read biographies of both. To the amusement of our parents, one day we shoved each other up and down the hall of our apartment like wrestlers as we argued. I still remember the tone of our silly spat.

"Leonardo painted almost nothing," Donnie said as he pushed me down the narrow hallway. "Michelangelo's are action-packed."

"Leonardo's paintings are perfect," I pushed back.

We danced into the living room, where our parents were attempting to read the *Herald-Tribune* or some other long-gone daily newspaper. Dwight Eisenhower was president, and maybe they were reading about his big new interstate highway proposal, or about how Democratic candidates, including John F. Kennedy, were throwing their figurative hats in the ring for the 1960 primaries. I say figurative because, though Ike always wore a hat, going hatless was one of the many ways Kennedy displayed his youthfulness and progressiveness, and that he represented a new generation.

We took a skidding turn in front of the parents. I'm sure we not only wanted them to see us but to be entertained at what we were arguing about. "Stop it!" Char said in her strong alto voice. "That's a direct order."

When Char gave a direct order, it had better be obeyed. She was a strong woman from a strong family. Her eyes did not line up because of a congenital nystagmus. So when she was really making a point, she would stare at you with just one. "It's the evil eye," Donnie, caught in a misdemeanor, would tell her jokingly. Her maiden name was well-known in Columbus. The family started a department store there in 1852. Lazarus was followed by Shillito's in Cincinnati and the business grew into Federated Department Stores, which included such leading names as Filene's in Boston and Abraham & Strauss in New York. Federated eventually turned into Macy's. People tend to assume that Macy's bought Federated. It was the other way around, but they used Macy's because it was more recognizable nationally.

In the Sixties, Federated's majordomo was Fred, the oldest of four brothers, and based, as was Federated, in Cincinnati. My new grandfather, Robert, was the youngest. I learned to call my grandfather Pop-pop, my grandmother, Hattie, Hoo-hoo, and Fred uncle. The nickname Pop-pop was quite usual. During the Second World War, Char and Warren left their newborn, Bobby, with Char's parents while she followed her husband to postings around the country. "Hoo-hoo", his grandmother would call down the long hallway. "Hoo-hoo," answered Bobby from behind his child gate.

Char's parents were getting up in years, and the apartment on 96th Street was too small for six people. There was talk of moving to the suburb of Riverdale. Char wanted to go home to Columbus. Dick, like me, considered it a different universe. The two of us couldn't imagine leaving New York City, "like living inside an electric lightbulb", as Truman Capote described it. Char was nothing if not determined. The arguments were long, noisy and sometimes scary. Char used her powerful force of persuasion. She won, of course, and they waited until I graduated from high school before moving. That was 1963. By then I'd gotten used to Columbus through trips in the summer and at holiday-time at my grandparents' stately white-painted brick house with its pool and cabana. My friends were all leaving town for college, too. That made it less heartbreaking. I rode my bike through Central Park one last time, through the rows of enormous plane trees you also see in the Tuileries Garden in Paris, trees said to represent sorrow. I photographed the bike leaning against a stone column at the seal pond in the zoo, with the seals swimming and sunning themselves against the glimmering Manhattan skyline.

It was an end, sad and bittersweet, and a beginning, full of unknowns.

Dick adjusted as best he could, becoming a character in *Future Shock*, a book about too much change in too short a period by Alvin

Toffler. In a chapter on the future of work called 'The New Nomads', a fellow named Bruce Robe, a "tall, graying Wall Street executive", had what was a novel commute, walking to the Wall Street heliport and taking the helicopter to the newly renamed Kennedy Airport. He flew TWA, now long-defunct, to Columbus, Ohio, where a car would be waiting at the airport. That was exactly Dick's weekly schedule: the heliport, Kennedy, TWA, Columbus and Char waiting to take him to our suburban home in Bexley in the red Buick Riviera. It took a few years, but gradually Dick spent less and less time in New York and more in Columbus, which, quite unexpectedly, he grew to love. So did I.

Following my grandparents' example, my parents spent winters at the La Quinta Resort and Club, a 1920s hotel. After discovery of a beneficent underground aquifer and the almost simultaneous diversion of Colorado River water, the grounds grew over the decades to a vast, impossibly green oasis in the stark, tinder-dry Southern California desert. La Quinta lies towards the end of a string of towns stretching south from Palm Springs. Grass, flowers and citrus trees blossomed and fruited. You could pick a grapefruit or orange off a tree for breakfast while walking from Char and Dick's rented house to the hotel and prepare yourself to be overwhelmed by the opulent non-native, water-guzzling impatiens, begonias and other flowers in February that Ohio was lucky to have by the late spring, as well as towering fountains and wide pools. The resort, a sprawling compound of red-roofed Spanish-style villas, was a bit of Versailles in the desert. For those who love golf or tennis, it was a destination, where Bruno Parvenus was the head tennis pro. He had faced Pancho Gonzales, a champion of the era, and purportedly gleaned games off him.

Bruno and the head of the riding stable had the idea of starting the Cherry Creek Tennis Ranch in Mancos, Colorado, and recruiting the children of La Quinta habitués. "Tennis is a lifetime sport," said Dick. And off we went.

The horses had arrived when the dozen or so campers descended on Cherry Creek, but as a 'tennis ranch' it lacked a crucial feature: a finished tennis court. The cement was laid. The court needed to be painted. Bruno set us kids to work with buckets of pine-green paint.

I'd never had to do anything much with my hands before, and it was a pleasure to learn to roll the paint smoothly onto the concrete. It was hot in the high-altitude morning sun, and before sunscreen was as sophisticated as today, so we were toasted. When we finished, we were tanned and deeply proud of our rectangle, precisely 78-feet long by 36-feet wide.

Bruno carefully inserted the white, straight lines to discipline play. A line on each side, 27 feet apart, distinguished the singles and doubles courts, the former narrower, creating two alleys. He made a 'T' on each side of where the net would go to govern when serves were in or out. Then the posts for the net went in, and the net itself was strung across the middle of the court. With a tape measure, Bruno adjusted the net to exactly three-feet, six-inches high at the posts and exactly three feet in the middle.

Now we could unscrew the presses on our wooden rackets and learn to shake hands with it, a traditional forehand grip. Bruno became a drill sergeant. He didn't drill us on form, finesse or strategy. The main thing we learned was to run to the ball wherever it was and return it as best we could. He taught a simple kids' serve— Western grip, so the flat of the racket faces the ball directly, and a low toss, which creates a leisurely but accurate arc. It was safe and a lot like my dad's serve. I developed a one-handed backhand, the norm at the time, that became my most dependable weapon.

Handball had been my game on the city streets in New York. It was perfect for neighborhood kids. Not only did the apartment buildings provide walls to bounce a rubber ball off, but the sidewalks marked off as squares could define a player's territory. Tennis was a natural extension, and I took to it happily. To Donnie's great frustration, I beat him every time we played. As we headed into August I could see my destiny. He was growing, and I was not. Once I lost, I would never win again. Our last match that summer Donnie had me, 5-0. It was over, except that he mentally left the court and lost the next seven games in a row. It was the last hurrah, the last time I beat him.

Donnie, the happy-go-lucky kid, grew to five-foot-ten over the next few years. In the Sixties, like many of us, he challenged the establishment, though he was not into politics as I was. It was more of a sex, drugs and rock 'n' roll rebellion. As a man he remained athletic, though his game of choice was not tennis but golf, which he liked to call 'goof'. Shockingly, over the years, probably when he became a parent, he switched direction and took on the role of a disciplinarian. He gave the next generation strong advice, delivered with our mother's conviction. Mean Uncle Donnie, as my daughter Wit called him, was always sure to tell me exactly what he thought, which could be painful. Later I became grateful. Few people were left who were willing to tell me something I needed to know.

Just as shockingly, Donnie mellowed after our parents died. Our sister Babette noticed it. "What's the matter with Donnie?" she asked me shortly before my malignant bigger-than-a-sunflower-seed subsumed my life.

"I think he's always been empathic, but didn't want to show it. Maybe a guy thing." He took on a family role that was watchful and caring, someone to count on.

Over the next 40 years, after Bruno's tennis camp, Dick would periodically hint that I would benefit from more tennis lessons. It was an annoying mantra. For most of that period, I had three growing children and a consuming full-time job as a researcher at Ohio State, first in water supply, then in telecommunications regulation. The best I could do for exercise was head out our front door and jog around the neighborhood.

"You could be as good as Babs and Mary if you worked at it," Dick would say. My aunts were tall, graceful women who played doubles with never-ending rallies, the balls arcing deep to the baseline over and over, the way a satisfying social doubles game was supposed to go. Mary, as I've mentioned, had to quit tennis by the time of this book but was still a dynamo. My aunt Babs—called Big Babs to distinguish her from my sister Babette and later my daughter Wit, another Babette—was gone. Wit began to use her middle name because she said Babette sounded like a French prostitute.

Big Babs and her gruff heart-surgeon husband Howard Sirak were serious art collectors. Howard was into exotic saltwater fish for a while before the two of them became obsessed with impressionist, post-impressionist and fauvist art. They accumulated Monets, Cézannes and Delaunays, and eventually left a world-class collection to the Columbus Museum of Art. One of their expressionist paintings by Jawlensky of a witchy green-faced woman in a lurid red hat, demurely holding a multi-colored fan, had become the museum's most-used icon.

Char and Dick's passion was the New York Yankees. Char had worked her way in as one of George Steinbrenner's limited partners when he bought the team in 1973. "There's nothing more limited than being a limited partner with George," she'd said. The partners had no involvement in decisions about the team. That was up to the principal owner and managing partner. But she was able to include Dick in the deal so he could join her for owners' meetings, and the two of them had a wonderful time sitting in the owners' box at the stadium through many baseball seasons. My siblings chose to take some of the ownership interest after Char and Dick died, but I declined.

When I was in my fifties and my parents in their seventies and telecommunications was in future shock with the development of the internet, giving me loads of work, Jack and I took a winter break to visit them at the La Quinta resort in the depths of winter. It would be warm, dry, and luxurious after grim, gray, not-quite-cold-enough-to-snow central Ohio.

Dick had talked regularly about quitting tennis. Golf was his preference by then. "I'm giving up the game," he'd say, lying on his bed with the pillow over his eyes. But he didn't. Courts got arranged by the pros; they always needed a fourth. Muttering that he was going to give up the game, my father would drag on his whites and drive to the courts. They were close enough that most of us walked, but he was saving his energy. My father played tennis until the year before he died, at age 83.

Dick bought me a lesson with the current pro, Mike Casey. By that point, I'd found time to play doubles indoors in the evening on a 3.5-level career women's team. That was high for club play. Rustiness would not be an excuse.

I hit with Mike, with the sky-scraping palm trees and ragged, pastel-shaded Santa Rosa Mountains looming beyond the courts.

Seeing my father sitting on a bench on the sidelines looking serious, I felt myself shrinking to far less than five feet, self-conscious, like a kid in the school play trying to remember her lines with her parents in the audience. A little of me resented the ludicrous situation. A little of me wanted to laugh. The rest of me was on a mission to nail the rapidly fed balls exactly the way Babs or Mary would. As I probably had from the time I was an infant and could smile up at his huge loving face, I wanted to please my dad. I know that look from seeing my own infants' unfiltered joy.

"You don't have to hit the ball as hard as you can on every shot," Mike said of my forehand. "Work on placement a bit."

"She could do that all day," he called to Dick as he fed me perfectly timed and placed backhands. They don't get fed to you in a match. Dick eased his serious face into a smile.

When we came to the serve, Mike saw an issue. "You need to work on your toss." He tried to teach me a rather elaborate serve.

Afterwards my father told me, "You were better than I thought."

Better than he thought means not good enough. I smiled inwardly as we walked back to the rental house, where Dick would boil artichokes straight from a field for lunch for Char, Jack and me. They were a staple at their winter home, and the only thing I ever saw him cook.

I have inherited traits from my father I didn't want. The deafness was his, a doughnut form that strikes in middle age. The nasty BRCA-2 gene was an inheritance, too. My need for athletics was from him. Dick was the goalie of the University of Virginia lacrosse team. I am nimble at the net. The fast reaction time descended to Wit, who played goalie for her high school lacrosse team. Once a local radio-show host, covering the big game between the Columbus School for Girls and the Columbus Academy, selected her as the city's high-school player-of-the-week: "Small but mighty," said the announcer. That's my middle child and me.

Recalling the lesson with Mike later, I decided "better than I thought" meant good enough. It made my father happy that I got the same kick from a social game he always enjoyed, an inheritance, the gift of movement.

11

NORTHAM PARK

A red-tailed hawk perching high in the leafy branches of one of the grand old sycamores of the city of Upper Arlington's Northam Park, relatives of the plane trees in New York's Central Park, would have seen a peculiar pattern on a tennis court below. Two dots on one side of the net repeatedly danced back towards the fence, apparently to pick something up in the gray area beyond the green-painted court, while the two dots on the other side didn't seem to move except straight between baseline and net. Sometimes there was a pause and the pattern would begin again, but with the two pairs of dots on the opposite sides of the net.

We'd lost at the Columbus Country Club. And they didn't serve cinnamon rolls. Warming up for the second match of the summer, my partner and I knew we were in trouble.

Our vigilant hawk would have had to perch much higher to locate herself in the greater world. She was in central Ohio, otherwise known as an insignificant dot in the 'great overfly' by residents of the east and west coasts of America and 'Chicago' by the rest of the world. Nor could she see, to the east, the suburb of Bexley, or beyond that Gahanna and beyond that Blacklick, an unincorporated township that Jack and I called home. We loved to get our mail posted

99

from the Blacklick post office. The P.O. stamp read 'boondocks', which was just fine. We were especially pleased not to live in New Albany, just north of Blacklick, with its endless showy McMansions and acres of boastful white fences.

"Why don't you move to New Albany?" people would ask us. Because Blacklick, a peaceful sliver of greenness out in the boondocks, was more our style. Our house was rustic looking inside and out, in keeping with the neighborhood. Windrush Creek, the first such planned community in Columbus, was built in the Seventies with the intention of creating an equestrian haven. For the convenience of the riders, walls and fences were forbidden and generous green common areas included. The horses never arrived, but the unfulfilled plan created a hidden gem in the clutter that sprung up around us. We were a haven where the fences were invisible, literally, since buried electric fences kept dogs on their own property. My dogs were too small to inflict with electric charges for the 'sin' of wandering. Predictably, as with any neighborhood, there were other invisible fences, too, as we struggled to reconcile being house-proud property owners and banding together to meet mutual needs.

East of the sharp-eyed, sharp-beaked hawk observing sideways from her perch, and west of Blacklick, New Albany, Gahanna and Bexley lay the most populous city in Ohio, 14th largest in the country, and second largest in the Midwest after Chicago. Columbus, at the confluence of the Scioto and Olentangy Rivers, housed the oddly roofless state capitol building, dozens of skyscrapers, apartment buildings and the spectacular Ohio Theater, a former movie palace. Downtown, that once housed the Lazarus department store, was still a bit of a vacuum compared to the Sixties, when my family moved to Bexley. Old-fashioned German Village boasted night-time entertainment as well as cobblestone streets. The Short North was as vibrant at night as a New York neighborhood (a very small NYC neighborhood) especially on gallery night, held once a month. Since I always faded out early, I didn't know if the Short North never slept.

When Wit was a resident after medical school, she was stunned to find her classmates thought of Columbus as an exciting destination for their permanent practices. She graduated from high school at the Columbus School for Girls with her greatest ambitions to escape her parents and her city. As a junior she lobbied Jack and me to let her head to the University of Alaska and skip senior year. She wanted the great outdoors. We managed to talk her out of that, telling her we wouldn't support anything west of the Mississippi. So she went to McGill in Montreal. We had not defined our geographical limits well. Wit headed to Canada for the international experience and found herself in the international dorm, where all the residents were Americans. It was a period when the Quebec government was trying to starve English-speaking McGill. Wit's classes had hundreds of students and negotiating with the administration was a constant nightmare. There were pluses: one dorm bottled its own wine. She experimented with a new look, shaving her head. Then she transferred to Bates, a tiny liberal-arts college in Maine where the professors and administrators were there to help and every member of the student body belonged to the outdoor club automatically.

Columbus, like other American cities, has its troubles.

Dick liked to say that the problem with Columbus was lack of a major league team in a major sport. Cincinnati and Cleveland had them, and all we had were the Ohio State Buckeyes, the cynosure of sports in the city, and an attendance of over 100,000 at every home football game. Another problem is that we perpetually have to add 'Ohio' to our name. 'Columbus,' I would state boldly, and pause, but people looked at me questioning.

Columbus has struggled with racial issues, especially out in the open in the last few years. Like Detroit and other metropolitan areas, the 2020s brought police violence and city-wide soul-searching. In 1992, we had proudly celebrated the landing of Christopher Columbus in the New World. The city mounted an expensive exhibition. Ameriflora, it was called, with zillions of flowers. Our housing development, Windrush, was able to buy the exhibition's fountain for our community pond. It became more and more uncomfortable to celebrate Christopher Columbus discovering the Bahamas, the first step in European ravaging of an Old World he knew nothing about. My solution is to change the name to 'Gahanna', the livable eastside suburb. It would reflect our aspirations and we would no longer have to say Ohio every time we said Columbus to an outsider. Gahanna, a Native American word for 'the joining of three waters', speaks to inclusiveness, a desirable concept in these parlous times. It would distinguish our city from the hanger-on Columbuses.

At Northam Park that summer day, my partner and I were destroyed, smithereened, strung up, bageled and hamstrung, winning zero games. We were sliced and diced to the size of the tiny openings between racket strings. We breathlessly chased serves that turned into aces, swished at lobs and caught glimmers of passing shots rocketing down our alleys. My partner was left-handed, so we hoped to cover the middle with our forehands. Hope had flown to the topmost twig of a sycamore tree.

Hope is a sneaky bastard, I mused driving the half mile to Josh's house after that latest crushing defeat to lick my wounds and play with my grandson. It's a Darwinian trait. Optimism is good for the survival of the species. If you tell yourself there are edible berries in the next break in the forest, you are more likely to make it through without starving, have children and pass on your hopeful genes. Don't trust that optimism is any good for you personally.

Is God a divinity up there in the sky, a holy Arnold Schwarzenegger like the muscular fellow depicted by Donnie's beloved Michelangelo in the Sistine Chapel? What a great fairytale. What about the afterlife? So many draw strength from a promise of eternal life. They're lucky. I couldn't help admiring them. Religion is the opium of the incurious.

12

ELYSIUM AWAY

The minimum age in the gold league is 50 and in the platinum league, 60. I signed up for both the former and the latter, brand new in Columbus in 2018, reasoning I would have more of a chance to win. That unforced error would soon be corrected.

The Elysium Tennis Club was a far cry from the elegant Columbus Country Club. Hidden away in an industrial park on convoluted back roads near a roaring state highway, the club was surrounded by companies that sold slabs of marble and granite in a desolate concrete wasteland. They employed fleets of noisy freight trucks that tainted the air with diesel fumes. Transmission lines soared overhead. The first time I played at Elysium, in a gold team match the year before, I got so lost driving there, even with GPS, that I was late. We had to forfeit court five, almost as humiliating as going 0-6, 0-6, the dreaded bageling.

My partner this time was Louise, the one who lived in the immediate present and days long past. As soon as I got there, she ambushed me. "Is this the last match of the season?"

"No, it's the first match in a different league."

We introduced ourselves to our opponents near the picnic table. We would be having lunchbox-sized bags of potato chips or

Fritos. Our enemies looked old and skinny in a lean and mean way. As we warmed up, what they looked was damnably strong. One was wearing green, so I would think of her as Diana Green; the other purple, so she would be Wendy Purple. It was a hard court, rather than our home clay, and the warm-up balls bounced higher than my head. I would have to stay back behind the baseline.

The court was painted blue but stained with reddish marks that looked as if they were made by balls. I couldn't figure out how a ball could leave that kind of rusty snail trail. No cracks or dips in the court, though. Well maintained. A tall fence, but it couldn't possibly block the view of the nearby transmission tower. A guy with average upper-body strength could probably hit the tower with a ball.

It was only nine o'clock in the morning, but the warm-up left me sweaty. I'd brought my own water bottle. Louise hadn't and someone kindly tossed one over the high fence. The plastic crushed but didn't break. We practiced our serves. One of the opponents bounced the ball twice with the slim edge of the frame of the racket before she served. Arthur Ashe practiced like that. I had never before seen a club player do it. *Uh oh*, I thought, *over 60 wasn't going to be enough.*

We popped open a can of balls. Their clean scent socked me with a dopamine rush. We took up our battle stances. Louise would receive. I bent my knees slightly in readiness to move in if her return passed the net player. Would we win a single game? Perhaps we should count our points instead. Green and Purple had to be women who once ruled the court. Their names were on plaques in clubhouses somewhere, champions in 1990 or 1980. They'd played on college teams. No longer limber, minus some horsepower, deprived of that last swift step that turns a drive into a rocket, they still had more than enough for the platinum league. These Elysiums were retired Valkyries, descending to earth to amuse themselves with mortals.

"Sometimes we go a little brain dead. So we all have to keep score," said one opponent. "With four of us, we ought to be able to figure it out."

Louise and I made it to deuce a few times. Perhaps the gods were taking pity. The Elysiums easily came into the net on our squishy returns. There they formed a wall like hulking transmission towers without the gaps. I tried going between Green and Purple. They had played together and knew exactly whose ball was whose. I tried going over their heads with lobs. One opponent would lift an arm high and take the fuzz off the ball. Louise stroked smoothly and solidly, but it wasn't enough.

At a break, I had no towel to wipe off the sweat pouring down my forehead. My soaked hair tickled my neck. The temperature must have already been in the 90s. The industrial smell of chemical fumes and diesel was stomach-churning and distracting. Louise and I poured cool water down our throats and looked at each other.

"The goals," I said, "have fun and try." But it was hard to have fun when you were being drilled into steaming cement.

I switched from my sunglasses to the clear ones, which had progressive lenses that let me see to the back of a tennis court on the top, focus on a computer screen in the middle and read a book in the bottom third. It took a couple of minutes to adjust. The sky was clear when we started to play, but now clouds scudded dizzyingly.

One point into the next game, I was no longer in the moment. I was not in any moment. A ball had wandered from a neighboring court, and as I walked under the swiftly running clouds to pick up the ball and shoo it back, I lost communication with earth. *Where was I? Elysium, Valhalla, Hades, Wimbledon?* I picked up the ball. Were we or the team on the next court playing with Wilson 4s?

"Isn't Wilson a basketball?" I asked it, looking down through the near-sighted section of my glasses. That didn't sound right. Louise had wandered over to the baseline as if to serve. But someone was facing me in the backhand court.

"I'm serving to you," said the lady in green. *Was her name Marlene?* Her words re-anchored me. I rolled the ball to the correct court, herded Louise to the forehand service line, took a couple of breaths and backed up to the baseline to receive the serve. At the next break, I chugged a long draft of warm water.

Being true ladies, the Elysiums started to call a ball in when it might not have caught the line, and perhaps they took a little off a return.

"I'm trying to keep it away from your backhand," said one of them kindly, making me want to smash a forehand into her midsection.

We were 0-5 in the second set. Maybe they would stop paying attention and focus on what groceries they needed to pick up after the match. Maybe they would collapse from the heat, and we would have to call the squad. I was used to dialing 911.

We savored our water, small bags of potato chips and some moist, delicious fruit under a small but shady tree. Tender chunks of watermelon, ruby-red strawberries and ripe cantaloupe. It reminded me of snacks on a break from a hike at summer camp. For five years, from the age of eight, I boarded a train in Grand Central Station with thousands of other kids and was whisked north, away from the gray skyscrapers of New York and away from the polio epidemic of the Fifties. My camp, tucked into the forested Green Mountains of New Hampshire, was Methodist. On Sunday, we donned white shorts with green buttons instead of the weekday green shorts with white buttons. If it wasn't raining, and it often rained, chapel was outside in the pine-scented summer air of New Hampshire, and we sang Methodist hymns. Once I was selected to read a poem to the congregation. I remember rising from my bench and nervously descending to the grassy chapel floor. Sunday evenings we had vespers, outside again. "Hark the vesper hymn is stealing o'er the waters soft and clear."

Crystal Lake, just beyond us and aptly named, lay calm and still.

13

SUNDAY IN THE SAUNA AT HOME

One Sunday morning late in June, we began our just-us-gals game in oppressive heat and humidity. Even the net shimmered with sweat. We moved in slow motion, taking long breaks. The perspiration poured down my face, clouding my glasses. My hatband was soaked. Ladies aren't supposed to sweat; we perspire. I stank like an unwashed teenage boy who hadn't figured out the deodorant thing. My ears filled with sweat under and around the hearing aids, dulling sound more than usual. I would be forced to ask other players what they said or to pretend I heard them and hope it wasn't important. My whites stuck to my skin. Helen, my partner, found towels. I soaked mine in cold water from the cooler and toweled my face and neck, then figuring it was only us, I toweled my arms and legs. I would have stripped if I could, flinging down the sticky, heavy bra packed with silicone and splashing my underarms in cold water. From a distance, though I could neither see nor hear it, I knew kids were bouncing off a diving board with excited laughs and splashes in a nearby pool. I imagined being immersed in cool blue water.

"Where are the balls?" asked Helen as we recovered sufficiently to start over. "I only have one."

The other two balls were huddled together in a remaining corner of shade. They had discovered an indentation in the clay that once was its own small river, but now, hard and dry as it was, could give little comfort. I wondered if they migrated south. "What's that?" one of my snowbird friends would say on the way to Florida. "A flock of geese?"

Desultory play resumed, with drives hit late off the back foot because the front one couldn't get ready and lobs that we watched and didn't chase. In or out, who cared.

A kerfuffle erupted on the second court. Edie had fallen and was lying flat on her back. Edie was someone I especially worried about. Some people get plumper as they age, and some thinner. Edie was the latter, thin as a racket handle. Braces embraced both knees. Nothing could stop Edie. She went for the ball like a Labrador after a rabbit. She stood up again and we resumed with a sigh of relief. The grip of my racket was sticky and I wiped my hand on my skort. Edie fell again. This time she didn't get up. The entire team gathered around, except for me. I stood back and observed because I wouldn't have been able to hear the conversation unless I stuck myself right at the front. At football games, you watch to see if the downed player is moving his legs so you can tell if he is conscious. Edie was moving and talking. They were all talking. She had fallen hard on her left hip. Someone helped her up and she limped towards me to sit on a bench. Her left arm was pocked with bruises. Extra bad luck since Edie was a lefty.

"I'm so sorry," I said. Someone had already given her water, so commiseration was all I could offer.

"You never know," she said.

Our wounded warrior was able to leave on her own, but I heard from Helen that the medical folks kept her in the hospital overnight because of worries about her head and neck. A week later, limping in pain, Edie came to a match as an observer. "I'm going to try to practice July 25th."

"That's next week."

"Better to go to practice and be able to leave. You can't in the middle of a match."

Injuries, illnesses and the inevitable aches and insults of aging may have slowed us down, but nothing could keep us off the court for long. Tennis was our constant, our obsession, our true love match. We were tennis ladies.

Years ago, a young woman at New Albany who carried the type of case that can hold four rackets said to me and my teammates, "I know your sort." She looked us up and down. "Cute clothes. Painted toes. No strokes."

"Painted toes? That's a bit harsh," I shot back. I looked around at my exceptionally quiet sneakered teammates, and realized some of them must indeed have beauty-salon pedis under their no-show socks. That was when I was still working at a research institute at Ohio State and didn't have time for beauty. After retiring, I succumbed to the pleasure of an afternoon having all 20 digits brightly painted.

We were tennis ladies. Of course, we sported cute clothes. New Albany required our costumes be 70 percent white. We flaunted the white rule with *élan*. Like a schoolgirl with a uniform requirement, I kept my eye out for outfits with vivid trim that would just catch the line.

We could be picky. After Sunday morning tennis, a few of us would go to lunch at the main clubhouse across the road. It was rejuvenating to sit outside at a white table adjacent to the closely clipped croquet court overlooking the velvety green of the golf course.

"I'll take a three-egg omelet with two egg whites and one whole egg," said one player, "and with spinach, mushrooms, Swiss cheese and chili peppers."

"I'll have Kent's Cobb salad with no chicken or bacon or eggs and extra Roquefort, avocado and tomatoes." (Kent Rigsby was the chef).

"Kent's Cobb salad with no eggs and extra chicken and bacon, and a ranch dressing on the side," said another.

I looked at our server, who seemed happy at the challenge. I wondered when a Kent's Cobb salad was no longer a Kent's Cobb salad.

We were self-aware. At another lunch, when my turn came around, I ordered the Cobb salad exactly as on the menu. Judy shot me an accusing stare. "You're weird."

"Remember the time the manager came over and asked 'is *anything* alright?'" said Ellen, a perfectly coiffed white-haired woman who was always composed in a match and had fantastic stories about life in Columbus from back when a short drive put you in the countryside.

We were achievers. The New Albany group that I began playing with 20 years before had several women who were raising families or not doing much except maybe real-estate brokering. Jack labeled them all New Albany princesses, which wasn't fair. My older group at the time of this story included a retired director of a mental-health clinic for children, a retired elementary school principal and other veterans of the workforce. I know I'm lucky, but didn't think I qualified as a New Albany princess, which implies someone who feels entitled, superior and taken care of by their husbands.

We were givers. I don't mean just volunteering at the museum. And the city did need art, along with everything else. We helped on the ground. Nan tutored kids with serious illnesses, like a five-year-old with a colostomy bag. "It makes you think," she'd said. We knew what kind of thinking. It was thinking about those children, and about how damned privileged we were.

We were almost always ladylike. We called an opponent's ball 'in' if there was any doubt. We deferred to the score that could easily be agreed on. We covered up the fervent desire for victory with layers of politeness worthy of diplomats reshaping borders in the Middle East.

There were exceptions, of course. Many years ago, I had a partner who was viciously keen on destroying the enemy. The pros had told us to talk to each other about strategy during a game, so she was bent on doing that after every point. There was little to talk about once we'd decided on a signal for poaching, where the net player zips sideways to cut off a service return.

"What should we do?" she might say, coming by for a secret confabulation.

"Get it over the net," I would say.

We were tied after the second set. Keeping track in tie-breakers was one of the banes of my existence. All tie-breakers have to be won by two points, but the number of points you play, who starts, how often you switch ends of the court and whether you have to break the tie in the first two sets or only the third (for women, since men may play five sets) differ by league. We agreed to play a nine-point tie-breaker. They won by the required two points.

"We could've played the third set," said my pissed-off partner. "Nobody else wanted the court." She angrily faced the player who had initiated the tie-breaker. Fearing fisticuffs, or at least a catty exchange of girly slaps, I stood between them, though they were tall enough that they looked over my head into each other's eyes.

"You're probably going to say you had to get back to your kids," yelled my partner into the woman's face.

"She does. She has a special-needs child and has to relieve the sitter," said her partner. The opponent broke into tears.

I've been known to be unladylike myself. I was playing with Debbie, the one who died of cancer. She truly had one stroke, a drop shot, and would hardly move. The pro told me to cover the court for her. I wasn't going to overdo that. Not only would it be unladylike, but beyond my ability to cover a whole doubles court. I couldn't cover an entire singles court anymore. But it was frustrating to watch her consistently short backspin returns. The opponents quickly figured them out and moved forward every time she hit the ball.

"Move," I barked in spite of myself in the middle of one point from behind Debbie, overtaking a shot into her territory that I was sure she could not make. I won the point.

Debbie walked back stroppily to where I stood on the backhand service line and hissed, "Don't you ever yell at me."

The red mist descended and I lost it, succumbing to a tantrum. The opposing server sent in a ball that I caught in my left hand instead of hitting back. Debbie couldn't see that from where she was positioned. The other team looked on, eyes wide, amazed and delighted to watch a full-blown meltdown. When my serve came around, I willed an effort. "Calm down," I told myself. The opponents were so shocked to see the ball come over the net that I won.

We flourished our 40 percent lavender or pink cute clothes well, edging over that 70 percent white rule. Sometimes we showed a little open back. We advertised the latest in scalloped skorts and sporty tights, the latter perhaps to stay warm or hide varicose veins or cellulite. Our hair may have been gray or white, but we colored it as we liked blonde or dark, as thick and beautiful as in high school, pertly tied back with bright bands. Or short and white (and chemo curly in my case), broadcasting our proud grandmotherly status.

We were bionic. We carried TSA notifications through airports to inform the authorities of artificial knees and hips. Rotator cuffs hadn't healed right, and we had gone to sidearm serves to ease the pain. One teammate had had three knees replaced. Ankles were sprained on the winter ice and the aches lingered into tennis season. Achilles heels lived up to their name; ditto, tennis elbows. We wore braces on arms, wrists, ankles, knees, calves and necks. We wore gauntlets on our hands. We taped sore fingers together. We wore clear glasses to protect our eyes after cataract surgery. One of us had to be accompanied to the bathroom to make sure she could find her way back. One of us had nerf balls for boobs.

Then there were the husbands. On average, men seem to break down younger than women.

Spending winters in La Quinta beneath the palm trees and perennial sunshine of Southern California as an adult, I was often invited to sub in a Sunday morning mixed-doubles game with three courts. Though many were into their eighties, the 11 other folks were probably great club players over the years. One Sunday morning my partner and I were walloping the enemy. He was fully into the game. He hobbled to a blooper at the greatest speed he could muster and returned the ball perfectly. "Marvin, did I see you run for a ball?" called his wife in a sharp, maternal tone from an adjacent court. "I don't want to have to take you to the hospital."

In Columbus, our team had husbands who were recovering from a kidney transplant, or in cramped housing in a nursing home with rapidly advancing Alzheimer's. One day the one with Alzheimer's, once a university economist, told his wife, also an economist, "I'm dead." She rolled her eyes and said, "You're eating a bagel and cream cheese. You're not dead." Then there was my husband, caged, cabined, cribbed and confined, with those twinkly blue eyes that spoke of younger times.

We had serviceable strokes and sensible serves. They may have been weaker than in past decades, but the direction and spin were intentional. It's court sense, a kind of wisdom that comes with age. We could size up opponents in the warm-up. We were wise to the usefulness of a lob into the backhand corner that younger players may not deign to try, preferring to propel their muscular bodies into the ball as hard as possible.

We were teammates. We played to win. But if it went the other way we still reveled in being fully present for those glorious moments in motion, for the sunshine, for the camaraderie and for lunch.

We were tennis ladies.

14

SCIOTO COUNTRY CLUB

The mercury crept up the thermometer like a centipede with a destination. Slowly wilting under a searing sun, we took a break from practice. I hot-footed it straight to the water cooler. Sven, the younger, or Junior, as his father Sven, also a tennis coach, sometimes slipped into calling him, was determined to teach even us. He had graduated from college only a few weeks before and wore a University of Toledo tennis T-shirt. I mentally thanked this earnest young man, with the flush of youth in his cheeks that his fashionable three-day-old beard could not disguise. He possessed the well-toned lankiness and golden skin of summer-long play. His thick, baby-fine eyelashes and doe-eyed enthusiasm were seductive. I laughed at myself for wanting to impress a lad somewhere between a quarter to a third my age.

"Be more aggressive at the net," said young Sven. "Finish it off."

I would do what this mesmerizing boy wanted as best I could. We brutalized a hundred balls or so, then collected them in hoppers or on our rackets, pouring them back into the basket cart. I claimed a hopper, holding it in my left hand to avoid extra work for the right and squishing the tennis balls lying tamely on the ground through the metal slats. "Ouch," one squeaked.

Surprisingly, the last drill included serves. I'd mentioned them to young Sven the week before.

"There's way too much to cover," he said, shaking his head. "You can practice that on your own." He was like my high school American history teacher in the Sixties who didn't have time to get to the Second World War, the most important event preceding my time.

It was more of a receiving drill than a serving drill. Two servers at a time were to hit second serves, meaning softer than the first. Sven wanted us to try three more aggressive responses than our usual hard crosscourt returns. Sven *père* paired me with Lynn. I didn't know Lynn's profession, or if she had one, but she reminded me of an elementary school teacher, a little plumper than she wanted to be, with the self-assurance of someone who could transform a room of third graders into obedient learners. Maybe she was a wee bit slower than once upon a time, but she was consistent. Sven didn't say for sure that she would be my partner at the Scioto Country Club the next morning, but I could hope.

A low wall that looked like it was hauled from New England, stone by stone, separated the Scioto Country Club from a busy city street. The club's discreet sign was barely visible. Wouldn't want to advertise a members-only institution dating from 1916, which was indeed getting to be a long time ago. The New Albany club opened in 1992, and even that was getting to be a while. New Albany's style was brick; Scioto's granite. I wound my way up a hill by banks of pink, purple, lavender, orange, scarlet and white impatiens and begonias, parked and found my team clustered under an open, white-painted structure by the courts. A machine dispensed crackly ice from one spigot and cold water from another into plastic cups emblazoned with the club's name and a list of major U.S. golf tournaments it had hosted.

"How many courts do you think we'll win?" I asked Bette, a good player, who was lounging on a white bench.

"None," she said, with the smile-wrinkles by her eyes fanning cheerfully.

Lynn and I were on court four. A promotion. I had a competent partner who wanted to play forehand.

I carefully remembered the names of our temporary enemies as Something Brunette and Something Blonde, then immediately forgot them. One of the opponents kept calling me Vivian every chance she got throughout the match, which started to feel like micro-aggression.

After losing 3-6 in the hard-fought first set, I wasn't bothered. The game embraced me. I was as one with the game of tennis, the tennis where I move and meet the ball on my terms and am aware only of a particular point in a pointilliste painting's universe. The opponents were whelming, not overwhelming, though they had a depressing tendency to reach even a pinpoint-placed ball, and, despite practice the day before, we had a meek tendency towards safe shots.

Two courts were already at the snack table as mine took an icy water break before the second set. I turned away from the others to adjust my weighty bra, which had slipped down below where breasts should be. Blondie hit a first serve into the net. A slow, juicy second serve came my way, and I spun it into an unreachable spot close to the net on the ad side, trick number one that Sven had taught us. I looked behind me, where players from courts one through three, their matches over, watched us. I sneakily gave my prostheses an upward tug. I shot Bette a big grin. Another second serve arrived, and I success-fully lobbed it into the deuce corner, trick number two. Unfortunately, as Judy, our eternally optimistic captain, would say, she managed to return it high and deep. Their game again. Court five finished losing its match and we paused as they trudged despondently past.

Game score 5-1, theirs. Brunette's serve. The only time you care about counting the number of deuces is when they go on forever, but you don't know that ahead of time. Trick three: a hard backhand down the alley. But the net lady was there. Ad out. Ad in. Ad out.

As the ladies of the Scioto Country Club finally finished us off, my brave partner said, "It must've been about 20 deuces."

"Sure felt like it," I said, helping myself to one of the two remaining heated breakfast burritos and a slug of lemonade. It was a victory to have deuces. It was a victory to be the last court to lose.

"Sven, did you notice I tried the second serve returns you drilled us on?" I asked, hoping for approbation. "What did you think about the match?"

He looked down at the face of his racket, giving me another opportunity to admire his eyelashes. Then he broke my heart. "It's about making good contact with the strings."

I stuffed the three yellow balls from the match back into their can. "Get the hell in there. No comments," I muttered to myself, zipping my snazzy new white-and-blue Head Instinct racket into its case. I wanted to slam the door to my car shut, but refrained.

Driving home, a memory of a Sunday doubles game a couple of years earlier crept in. It had been getting cooler and the outdoor courts collected leaves faster than they could be picked up. Time to move inside to the indoor courts at Scarborough East. One player brought pink balls from a breast cancer-awareness fundraiser. She opened the can with a snap and a fizz. Warming up, we immediately lost one of the brand-new, easy-to-see balls. People on adjoining courts denied seeing the stray. The four of us looked behind every one of the tarps that hung from ceiling to floor on three sides of our court, lifting and shaking the heavy, oily-smelling plastic and peering behind it at the dust-covered floor. A door was open in one corner, so I walked outside into the glaring sunlight. It took a moment to adjust my eyes. A couple of old, ratty-looking yellow balls lay partly buried in the grass. Nothing pink.

Nobody could remember the ball disappearing.

"Maybe it decided to escape," I said, drifting into fantasy world. "Or maybe a drone flew in, grabbed it and spirited it away." I'd never mentioned my habit of playing with the idea of the tennis balls as a kind of Greek chorus, figuring it was a bit weird. "The drone could have a pair of little clamps, and it would pinch the ball in its grip."

The other three players shot knowing glances at each other.

"It's a joke," I said.

Relief softened the women's faces. They looked at me and tried to laugh. *Sane, thank goodness*, they were probably thinking.

My mind took off.

A hand popped the can open with a snap and a fizz. Out leapt May, Kay and Fae, bright pink and perfumed with new ball smell. Bounce. Thwat. Bounce. Thwat. The rhythm of the warm-up. The game would soon begin and the balls would see how good these players were. May hoped she would be made to spin like a ballerina, forcing mis-hits. Kay longed to find that sweet path down the middle, between teammates. Fae thought the quartet of old ladies looked like lobbers. She anticipated reaching the ceiling and bouncing off a light, causing a let. That's what happened, except for hitting the light. The lob went long and Fae found herself flying out the open door, uncanned and unconfined. Fae chose to go higher, above the farmer's market where she could see apples, pumpkins and bizarrely shaped squashes spilling out of baskets. She was designed for topspin and backspin and it was dizzying to control yaw and pitch. She could hear a siren that grew louder and dipped down to investigate. A truck with a red cross on the side was pulling into one of the long, white building's entries.

A hospital, thought Fae and began a slow descent, curling around the flat roof to look in the windows. In one, overflowing with helium balloons, sunflowers and chrysanthemums, she saw a patient upright in bed petting a therapy dog with a hand from which jutted an IV pinned down by wide tape. Machines beeped and buzzed. What appeared to be his whole family—wife and three small children—were gathered around chatting and laughing.

Through another, she saw a bony old woman lying on a white-sheeted bed. The room was quiet except for her ragged breathing. No artificial lights, only the faint sunlight from the window. Fae wondered if she was ever a tennis player. She thought about how the ancient, still woman could have learned tennis because her father said it was a lifetime sport.

Hovering was more difficult than flying, and Fae needed to move. Down to earth was not a choice. On the ground she would disintegrate, or be picked up by a Labrador who would play her to shreds. In the air she would be free but without purpose. Should she fly back to the indoor tennis courts and rejoin May and Kay?

May and Kay were doing the work of three. Bits of pink fuzz littered the court. The tennis ladies were engrossed, aware only of the next point, the steady back and forth, the baseline, service line, doubles lines, and the first enemy of tennis players—the net. May and Kay were full of joy to be doing their jobs. It was a church where the hymns don't promise salvation, only the salty sweat of the game.

I have promises to keep, thought Fae, holding still in the hot summer air one more minute to look at the woman who had no more promises.

15

ELYSIUM HOME

If Louise didn't make it by match time, we would have to forfeit to Pauline and Barb. Somehow I was remembering their names. Barb was all legs and teeth. Pauline was close to my eye-level and strikingly skeletal with skin that looked as thin and transparent as cling film over her sharp bones. Just when I thought it would be better to forfeit, Louise appeared accompanied by a woman in uniform. Lightning lit the clouds northwest of us, and it began to rain, not sheets but a determined sprinkle. Young Sven explained that the rain wouldn't make the court unsafe but would kill the balls. He had us wait a few minutes, huddled under the umbrella between courts until it stopped spritzing. The court was grainy but dry enough.

Our team was firmly mired at the bottom of the league. Judy, our captain, was constitutionally optimistic, lean and leggy with a fashionably caramel-highlighted mane and a toothy Kennedy-esque smile. By the end of the season Judy's post-match emails were walking a line. She used words like 'fantastic' and 'awesome', tempered by 'great effort' and 'lots of deuces', and, in admission of facts, 'nonetheless', 'unfortunately' and 'sadly'.

I was so late on one return of serve that I flayed the ball over the fence and into the thick jungle of bushes. I noted the slat it jumped over and on a change of sides trotted through the gate and around to the wall of sweet-smelling, piney greenery. The wet needles pricked my bare arms and legs as I struggled through the bushes towards the outside of the fence. The branches rained on my head. Nestled between the fence and bushes lay a long row of grizzled tennis balls. Some had been there so long they had been bleached white by the sun. I hadn't known we had a gallery. Facing the fence from the non-court side, I couldn't identify the correct slat. Luck was with me, though, and I snagged our bright, fuzzy Pro Penn, which was perching in the evergreen branches. "Enough with trying to hide," I told it.

"Are we in the first set?" Louise asked.

"No. It's 1-4 in the third set. We decided to keep playing since the first two were over so quickly."

We hadn't played too badly. We had long rallies. We had deuces. But my serve was off. I couldn't toss it straight up. It wavered to two o'clock, or maybe three. It wavered to ten o'clock or maybe nine. It was too far in front; too far behind. I held the ball out at arm's length and raised it high to coax some hope out of the air.

"Second serve first," advised one of my fellow players. There are periods when all my serves are second and I was into one. Opponents eat them up like servings of dim sum.

The serve is the most important stroke in tennis for any level of player. With one downswing that is entirely up to you, your opponent is on defense. Even in easy-going social tennis, it's vital not to double fault. A double fault means you have failed to get a point started. Nobody can have any fun. A marshmallow serve knocks you on to the defensive, inviting drop shots or lobs that creaky limbs have to pump to reach or making your partner angry as the ball comes back in her face. My serve was veering towards entropic randomness, and I was reduced to holding my racket up and making a low, tentative toss, a ragged, two-step process that might get the ball in play but was way too easy to angle back or lob.

So it was that on a cool morning in the waning days of August, that maniacally active year of 2018, as a few yellow leaves drifted from the locust trees by the tennis courts, I approached young Sven for a serving lesson, the latest in decades of attempts to get a crackling good start on the game in the doubles rotation where I had the most control. I would try one more time for a consistent delivery hard enough to keep the opponent back at the baseline.

Sven, with his youthful energy, was eager to help. He wanted to teach in half an hour everything I still needed to know about the tennis serve after a half century of playing the game. He changed my stance and my toss, down to where on the ball to place my left pinkie. "Remember to practice," he told me. "And if they come in on you, aim straight for their bodies."

I was on my own again. How much would stick in a head that didn't always remember the score? How much would my muscles remember? What were the chances that I would clutch and fall back on second serve first in an actual game?

I checked out a hopper of balls to practice. The guy at the shop asked, "What court would you like?"

"One where no one can see me." That was court four or five, the ones surrounded by bushes. The wizened white tennis balls would observe, but nobody else. I hit 50 balls on one side of the net, 25 to the forehand court and 25 to the backhand, then went over to the other side for another 50. On my own, with no one watching, most of the balls had zing and direction.

The following Sunday, Labor Day weekend, when summer suddenly lost its glint, I stuffed my snazzy new racket and New Albany cap in the back seat, pressed the ignition button and was off for a casual morning game. I wondered why I was bothering. Why couldn't I quit like my friend Jody, who accompanied me on that first course of chemo? Was it mostly to escape from my sad home and my responsibilities for my patient? Home sounded pretty good right that minute. I could have settled on the screen porch, sunk deep into the cushy sofa, reading the Sunday *Times* with a cup of coffee and a Pom on each side, while Jack took in *Meet the Press* in the family room. Maybe the arts section reviewed a new TV mystery series.

Outdoor courts were beginning to collect leaves faster than they could be picked up. The yellow jackets were back. You could tell when you saw a player flailing with her racket at something unseen or when your arm was tickled by what you knew were the delicate feet of a fiercely territorial insect that would sting if it got riled up. You can't call in sick, though, when you are one of eight players. Getting away from my house, half of which was rigged out like a nursing home, was part of the point. The adrenaline would boost my mood and the company would be cheering. My father didn't quit. I wouldn't either.

"They're not takin' away my shot," I sang to myself loudly and with rap emphasis. I danced the red beamer into a spot near the pair of courts banked by tall bushes and taller evergreens, thick and lush from an unusually rainy summer.

The usual gang was at the club except for a sub for Helen, whose husband was recuperating from a kidney transplant. I knew he was on dialysis, but not that he was eligible for a transplant. We chattered and drew our cards. I had the four and Edie the three. We were partners.

"Why don't I play backhand?" Edie suggested. A lefty was saying, "I am stronger than you and will do the hard part."

Ha, no way. Little does she know that young Sven has given me the keys to the universe.

The opponents won the toss and decided to serve first. When our turn came, Edie would serve facing west, so she would not be looking into the sun.

On the first point of game one, I returned the ball into the net. On the next point, Edie returned at an angle past the net player, my signal to move in from the service line. The server made a soft, high return. I jumped two inches into the air, reached the ball and slammed it between the opposing players with a satisfying thump. *Oh, the grat-ification! The thrill!* I was five-feet-six inches tall. I was powerful. I was guarding the lacrosse goal. Fifteen-all. I returned the serve into the net again and did a McEnroe, hammering my racket's edge on the ground once. I would have done it twice, but it hurt my wrist.

Inevitably, the dreaded turn to serve arrived.

With the edge of my racket, I drew a half circle at the baseline, planning to toss the ball so that if it were not hit it would fall smack inside the mark. I placed my left foot carefully a half inch behind the baseline and pointed it towards the right-hand net post. I called to mind the four tennis balls Sven placed on the ground in front of the baseline to show the arc my right arm should make coming around after it met the ball for a flat serve. I would lift with the middle of my fingers, not the tips. I would be sure to lift my pinkie along with the other fingers. In a single motion, I would draw back the racket behind my head with the flat facing my curly hair and bring it around and through the ball over the imaginary X at 1:00 in front of my feet and over the half circle and finish with my racket face down pointing towards my opponent's body.

That opponent, halfway to the service line, swished her racket from side to side like a cobra in anticipation of a luscious mongoose.

The toss was too far to the right. I let it bounce. Next try. The toss was over my head, which would be fine if I still owned a twist serve. I caught the ball. This was a sociable game and my sociable friends were waiting patiently. Toes, left arm, fingers, pinkie, X, right arm, racket face, arc, finish.

Serve the stupid ball. This is my shot.

The toss was off, but in a Zen moment I moved my feet a couple of inches and hit anyway. Blip. In. Blap. Back to my dependable one-handed backhand, and I sent it hard down the middle past both players and just short of the baseline. A perfect shot.

I played with the game I had, and it was sufficient. It was glorious. I won points. I lost points. I was in Nirvana or Elysium. It was my serve again.

"It's 11:30 already," said another player. Ending time.

"11:28," I said. "We could get in another."

Don't let this be over. Just one more game.

I had survived a full year without cancer. I'd played through it. It had been as good a 12 months as it could be. As I looked back, I realized how much I'd thought about religion, hoping to get some, I suppose. Buddhism, Methodism, even the God on the ceiling of the Sistine Chapel had something going for them. It struck me that I may have learned a few lessons, or at least been reminded of truths about human life well lived.

In the United States religion is a capitalist market with billboards for everything from Jews for Jesus and evangelicals speaking in tongues to the traditional pillars of religion—Islam, Judaism, Christianity. As long as religions are tolerant of other versions of the game, they make lives richer and help people be good human beings. So many choices. You'd think I could pick something.

My parents were Jewish, but didn't practice it and didn't encourage us to learn a thing about it. I call myself a non-practicing Jew. It's an exaggeration. I've attended only a few bar mitzvahs and bat mitzvahs and the confirmation of one niece who somehow decided to go with the program. We celebrate Passover each year, and I cook a genuine meal. We do the whole megillah with a Haggadah that emphasizes how we, the Jews, were slaves in Egypt. The value taught is freedom, though the story has a whole lot of vengeful god in it. And the menu is delicious. I wanted Vincent to have a Jewish history in his heart along with the non-practicing Catholicism of his mother's family.

Dick's family helped establish the Ethical Culture Society in New York City. Like many religions, it provides a structure for moral striving. Let's be kind to each other and try to be better people. The Golden Rule is the big one, and central to religion's ethical culture. The big benefits of organized religion are a team and rules—community and a moral framework. I like teams. I like rules. I like clear boundaries.

On rate toujours sa vie, du moment qu'on meurt, wrote Jean-Paul Sartre in *Les Jeux Sont Fait*. The game is up the moment you die.

Tennis, like roulette, is a distraction, a comforting routine before the game is up.

Yet, willy-nilly, I had a new perspective and my new life was more spacious, calmer and gentler. The brush with mortality, like other shocks and seismic changes, some of them for the better, pressured me to take a snapshot, in the midst of things, at past and future. Those dark, soul-searching nights had instilled a deeper welcome to happiness. The darkness would come back when it was ready. I counted five lessons learned, or more likely relearned with greater depth.

MOVE. I was headed the same way as Jack, one way or another. Throat muscles that couldn't contract in a swallow were another step in the journey, a downward step, but one that could be dealt with. Maybe. Could I be as brave? If you can't run anymore, walk to new destinations, far-off, mysterious places you never thought of. Ride on a cruise ship if you have to. They won't be as much like waiting rooms if that's all that's left. If you can't walk, and are strapped into a wheelchair so you don't slide off, let your mind run, figure out what it's saying and pound your keyboard with words. If you can't bash your keyboard, enjoy your monkey mind. Howler monkeys chattering and clicking and waking up the countryside seem to have a good time. Why do they get a bad rap? Take what's left, like Jack does, and watch.

LOVE. When I was in peanut treatment it was embarrassing how greedy I was for all forms of comfort. In the future, when a friend or relation is ill, I would go an extra step. Where I might have skipped the note, I would send one. Where I would have sent a note, I would send flowers or food. Where I would have paid a call, I would visit bearing hyacinth bulbs, brisket, home fries, green beans, apple pie and a feast of distracting, ordinary conversation. Even if people weren't physically ill, I would be more present for them. In the wider world, I would be a better philanthropist. Altruism is intensely self-aggrandizing. Generosity, valued by Buddhism and other religions, affirms not only ourselves, however. It's self-interested, but the self-interest of a humble self that has internalized and accepted hardship and loss. I would understand that giving, the non-judgmental, attentive sort, strengthens us all.

BREATHE. Not like you're about to go into one more room and climb onto an examining table. You don't have to close your eyes, hide in an ashram or find exactly the right pillow to sit on then drive away all thought according to a formula. Though that's one approach. There are many ways to pause from stifling or overwhelming routines. Poetry is one. Read a poem you like. Then read it again, and again until it permeates your heart. Find your own silent place, like my view of Windrush Pond. Is the great blue heron in for a feeding this morning? Sit with your beloved and count the blue jays and downy woodpeckers at the bird feeder, the nuthatch feeding upside down on the pole, the purple finches and house sparrows diving in for their share. Bless each Pom with a communion wafer in the form of a hard rawhide treat and marvel at how they use their paws to hold the delicious sticks firmly while gnawing hard and loud.

LIVE. Skid sideways on the clay and pound that ball. If you miss it, yell "I've got it" and ease the next one down the middle like time's arrow. Drink life like Gatorade is champagne. Drink champagne, too. Play the game with champagne in one hand and a cinnamon roll in the other. Trust that there is a life force stronger than entropy and you are part of it.

LAUGH. Most of all, laugh. Laughter is movement that assaults humbug. It's like internal tennis. Laugh with your friends because it brings you closer. Love the people who laugh with you and savor your connection. And laugh to yourself at the man or woman who seeks the theory of everything. Laughter is special breathing, relaxing your internal organs with a chortle or a giggle and, of course, the laughter that unexpectedly takes you by storm and sends you rolling on the floor. Laughter is free medicine. It's sunshine that breaks through the gloom and sends it scuttling back into the shadows. Laughter distances you from the hurly burly, putting you in panoramic rather than portrait mode. Especially learn to laugh at trials and troubles before you're old, so you have plenty to laugh at in your so-called golden years.

You may not agree with my choice of humor as the most important factor enriching old age. Maybe you'd start somewhere else and come to a different conclusion. Maybe you'd add something else, like 'learn', which in this little list of late-life lessons has the literary leverage of leading with an 'L'. The value of learning is not absent, however, but subsumed in the other cheery verbs attempting to boil down three score and 15 years of experience. Humor is the essential oil that soothes the human condition, the silken rope that binds us. I'm offering a practical, not a scientific tool. And it is emphatically not intended as a to-do list, more a collection of nourishing attitudes.

As the great philosopher Pogo Possum said, "Don't take life too serious. It ain't nohow permanent."

16

GAME OVER

I was in my loft office, alternately gazing out at the ominous, gray sky and skimming the news on my iPad, when Steve shouted for me. I dashed into the bedroom. Jack couldn't raise his right arm. His breathing was shallow and ragged. Our devoted home caregiver was struggling to pull him up into a sitting position in bed for a transfer to the wheelchair and then his shower.

Steve looked up at me, panicked. "I think he's had a stroke."

With painfully deliberate speed, we conducted the FAST test for stroke, leaving out the 'A' which asks whether an arm is weak. Jack's face wasn't noticeably crooked. His lips always curled down a bit on one side. Face was as usual.

"Repeat Mary had a little lamb."

"Mary had a little lamb." His speech wasn't slurred.

We added a question to check on confusion: "What month is it?"

"Umm, June."

It was Wednesday, February 12, 2020. 'T' is for 'time' to call 911. Five large technicians, two more than usual, including a broadly built female, barreled into our bedroom. Jack gave his crooked grin that said *here we go again*.

"Take him to the Ohio State ER," I said.

"That'll cost extra," Steve pointed out. Mount Carmel, where Russell had served as a four-legged therapist, was much closer.

"Ohio State," I insisted. It was a direct order.

The doctors did indeed have fixes for repeats of the tuna-fish episode that provoked a call to 911 over Christmas. It was one of those things that is routine for them but fit the Ohio State billboard campaign: *There is no such thing as routine blepharitis.* A physical therapist helped Jack with swallowing exercises. The neurologist prescribed a soft-food diet with thickened liquids. A powder the consistency of honey was to be stirred into anything he drank. Jack, eager to return to our pre-crisis lives, was okay with that except for his evening wine. He refused to thicken a Bordeaux or Fumé Blanc. It was interesting to see how little wine he drank, however. A couple of sips and the glass would sit three-quarters full. Wine was an embedded habit, and even if he didn't drink much, he liked to have it on his tray. The practitioners made the new diet sound ordinary, and the coughing spells were gone. MS is a slow road down, but the grade is often gentler than a hill in the Midwest.

The previous spring, soft-shell crabs, a favorite of Jack's and mine, arrived at the New Albany club from Maryland. I found a wide-enough handicapped parking spot, pressed the button to open the sliding side door and let down the ramp behind it. Jack unlocked his wheelchair from its slot on the passenger side and positioned himself to shoot down it like a skier out of the chute. He was off without me, excited about the soft-shell crabs. Back when he could walk, Jack had the annoying habit of striding off far ahead of me on tourist adventures. Now it was endearing to see him pushing the chair's toggle all the way to set a smart pace.

New Albany served the crabs breaded, but I had called ahead to ask for the buttery, saucy *meunière* style, which we liked better. At our usual table, Jack asked the waitress to tell the kitchen to cut up the crabs. The plates arrived, mine with two whole crabs on their backs. I watched happily as Jack slowly speared bits and brought them to his mouth with a shaky hand.

A few months later, it started to help if I fed Jack directly. It was a task that ate up an hour at a time. Jack enjoyed it immensely.

He looked at me like a six-month-old tonguing something sweet like mashed bananas. I ached at how demeaning this ought to be for him. I started to avoid looking at my husband's beautiful eyes that had shared so much happiness. I wanted to be at my desk or on a tennis court or anywhere else but this humiliating ritual of having to spoon-feed my husband.

"I refuse to feed you at a restaurant," I told him. He nodded. I wasn't sure that he found the idea embarrassing, more that he could see it would be odd. One evening we went out for dinner with Donnie and Lisal, and Jack ordered the bruschetta cut up. He stabbed at the pieces of bread, spilling onion and tomato across the plate. In despair, I took over the fork while my brother and sister-in-law quietly looked on. It hurt that they had to watch my husband's degradation, but Jack didn't seem to mind. It was one more thing to deal with. Along with his physical decline, his vision was worsening and he seemed a little loony, not keeping track of things.

Feeding tubes, the ultimate medical treatment for hard-to-treat swallowing, had always been our symbolic marker to stop treatment, give up, say enough is enough. Doctors can always do something more down to the last days. But liquid nourishment through a tube for a practiced gourmand and oenophile would mean there was nothing left in life to enjoy. Neither of us wanted extraordinary measures to keep us as alive as an eggplant, or so I thought.

We had consulted Wit on an end-of-life plan a couple of years earlier when she was in town. She and her husband Gideon had moved to Phoenix, where she was an emergency physician at St. Joseph's, one of the city's larger hospitals.

The three of us gathered around the kitchen table. Wit leaned in on her chair, looking businesslike. "Okay, right now you are DNR, Dad. That's 'do not resuscitate'. That means no CPR, no electric shocks to the heart. When you call 911, the team won't try extraordinary measures. Without a DNR, the ambulance team will administer CPR, try to kick your heart back to beating, until they get you to the hospital. The docs will then consult you, Mom, on next steps if Dad can't."

Jack pressed the issue. "So with a DNR, no further decisions will be made until the hospital?"

"No."

"A doctor won't be the one in charge when CPR is or is not started?"

"No. But you should know what the odds are. Almost all those resuscitations fail. Nationally about two percent of people who get CPR outside of a hospital survive, and those that do are unlikely to leave the hospital in a condition similar to before they went in." She meant they would probably be closer to eggplant status.

"Also," she continued, "there's DNI. That means 'do not intubate', no tubes down the throat. With DNR/DNI you can still get medications, like antibiotics, or have procedures or potentially life-saving surgeries. Next is 'comfort care' and after that hospice, though they overlap a lot. You know what hospice means. Comfort care is medical support, but not antibiotics. You can have meds, especially for pain and things like nausea, but the goal switches from doing everything to keep you alive to everything to keep you comfortable, which may mean what you associate with hospice care, allowing a comfortable but natural death."

Jack was mostly silent, though he nodded a couple of times. I wondered what he was thinking.

"We have living wills," I reminded them both. "They say there shouldn't be any medical intervention if it's a hopeless state."

"And what state is that?" Wit asked. "Everyone's definition of a hopeless state is different. A person is always allowed to change his mind. And the doctors go by the DNR if you have it with you, or will 'do everything' in its absence." A living will was not the document that told doctors what to do next.

Jack didn't like the idea of pre-hospital staff making the decision on allowing his life to end. "I want them to take me to the hospital and have the doctors decide there." This was a new twist to me, and I didn't consider the implications. How much trauma would he really want to endure in the weeks or days when death was inevitable?

"You're saying you don't want a DNR order," I confirmed with Jack.

We did not file a DNR order in Ohio State's computer system. This was a crucial decision that may have led to exactly what I thought we had been avoiding by having living wills. My husband lost everything but his heroically hopeless will to live.

In the last few months of Jack's life, his body fell apart in shocking ways. But it wasn't the weak throat muscles that precipitated the final, excruciating roller-coaster ride. Infections of various kinds had been among our greatest fears from the time MS wrestled him into a wheelchair. Among them, urinary-tract infections had become exceptionally risky when Jack finally decided to have a suprapubic catheter installed, that is, a plastic line into a hole below his belly button that would draw out urine into a bag that could hang on the edge of the bed at night. In the daytime, a smaller bag could be discreetly hidden under his trousers. Neither of us understood the risk of a perpetual hole in the body that was guaranteed to transfer pathogens.

At first the UTIs were one more thing. Jack would develop a fever. Steve and I would get him to the urologist's office. Weak and old people like Jack (and probably me) don't necessarily spike a fever, however. Confusion, the sort Jack had after his 2010 cancer surgery, is a common symptom. At the ER that February day, far, far from what Jack thought was June, the docs found no evidence of a stroke. They suspected the latest of many urinary-tract infections. Based on that guess, they started an intravenous infusion of a shotgun of antibiotics that went after many types of UTIs. Jack and I spent an afternoon and evening in the hallway of the ER. He was admitted to a spacious room on the eighth floor of the Ohio State Brain and Spine Hospital. It became his home and mine.

Remembering the mistake I made not hiring an overnight sitter when Jack had his sinus surgery in Pittsburgh, I slept in the hospital the first night. It wasn't strictly necessary. He couldn't press the call button to summon help but various wires connected directly to the nurses' station. The couch folded out into a bed. I brought two blankets and a pillow. The foldout was over five-feet long, just right for little me. I took out one hearing aid, the one that would otherwise lie on a pillow and squeal. I slept in snatches.

After that, I arrived early the next couple of mornings and Jack and I watched CNN. The World Health Organization was warning of "a public health emergency of international concern," a virus that seemed to have originated in China. The United States had banned entry for travelers who had recently been there.

The diagnosis was indeed another UTI. At least one of the antibiotics seemed to have kicked in and Jack had no fever. Steve and I fed him small bites of mashed slop the hospital called food and plied him with apple juice. He had enough energy to wave his arms around and bob his head up and down the way he did after the nose surgery a decade ago. I started to feel like we were going to escape one more scare. Unfortunately, he was a bit wacko, delirious again like the Pittsburgh experience.

"Give me my iPad," he demanded, with a scalding stare. "It's on the floor."

"I took it home for safekeeping."

"It's on the floor. Get it." Mouth carved into a frown, he paused long enough to catch his breath before continuing angrily. "Get me my iPad."

"It's not here."

"It fell off the boat." He was furious at me for being so stupid and unhelpful.

"Really, your iPad is fine." It wasn't as if he had the strength or motor control back to use a tablet. It would simply be a comfort lying on his chest.

"I want my iPad."

"I have it. It's safe," I said gently, but he was defiant.

"No, you don't. And it's not waterproof." I was being impossibly dense.

"Look, I've tried every way I can to tell you that the iPad isn't here. It hasn't fallen off the boat or into the water. I told you I have it to make you quit harping on about it."

He stopped. I was surprised.

Jack was still not eating well, despite our efforts to push soup into his mouth. The nurses couldn't get his pills in either. Without his anti-spasmodic drug, his legs would flail about in pain. Leg spasms are a wretchedly uncomfortable symptom of MS.

"We can put a temporary tube in his nose to get the medications in," Dr. O'Dorisio, the attending hospitalist, suggested. Ruddy-cheeked and cheery, he said his philosophy was practical nihilism, meaning not doing something unless it was necessary. I didn't point out that nihilism isn't about doing nothing; it's about not caring about a damned thing. Surely he meant 'do no harm'.

Without the tube up the nose, Jack would be a miserable shaking wreck likely in terrible pain. I was thinking of nothing else. I authorized the harm.

Later that day someone told me Jack wasn't getting enough nutrition. "We can go ahead and feed him through the tube."

I authorized liquid food through the nose.

Wit called that evening for her daily briefing. I said her father was getting his meds and food through a tube.

"What kind of tube?"

I told her.

"Mom," she said, alarm buried under a professional tone, "nothing up the nose."

Oops.

"He has no cribriform plate."

"No what?"

"The protective thing between the nasal passage and the brain. There's nothing but a flap of skin there now. Don't you remember that in Pittsburgh they said never to put anything up the nose?"

Oh, shit. I'd forgotten and had been thinking of his immediate comfort. Also mine. I'd seen his legs shaking uncontrollably when he was undermedicated. And he needed sustenance.

"There was no injury to the brain putting it in?" she asked, assuming the answer.

"No."

"Then that's that. They did a good job."

On Thursday of that nightmare week, Marty, Rachael's pastor husband, visited the hospital room. Jack was asleep, oblivious, his mouth wide open. We talked a bit, and Marty asked if he could say a prayer. I agreed. It was a kind gesture that would do no harm and maybe ease the constant anxiety begging to burst out in fruitless rage and uncontrollable tears. I cry rarely. When I do, it's a deluge that has to take its course.

We stood and Marty held my hands with his. He closed his eyes, and I closed mine to hear about relying on Jesus. The prayer, probably millennia old, reached my anguished spirit and calmed me. Just as Marty was finishing up, Jack's best friend Bob, who is observantly Jewish, walked in. Startled at a scene of Christian prayer, he backed up so as not to interrupt. When Marty was done ministering to Jack and me, I introduced him to Bob.

After Marty left, I explained the relationship and what Rachael meant to Jack and me, and the extraordinary carer she was. Bob hefted himself onto a chair and placed his hands over his large belly. He introduced the topic, sports. The Astros weren't doing anything new by stealing signs, just modernizing the methods, and it wasn't cricket to punish them. By that he meant that the game is baseball, not cricket. It was fun to be in one of our lively discussions for a few minutes. Quick-witted and clever, Bob was great company and a hell of a friend, even though he is fiercely conservative. We never talked politics. It was off the table.

"They're trying to get him to rehab," I said to Bob quietly.

Bob looked at Jack, then at me. *You're kidding* he said with his eyes and then in his booming voice, "Good luck with that."

"He can hear you," I whispered, knowing that was something you watch out for with a patient like Jack. Hearing is the last sense to go. He'd lost the ability to smell and much of his sense of taste from the nose surgery a decade before. He had no sense of touch in half his body. His eyesight was failing so he couldn't read. He was like the knight in a Monty Python movie who first gets one arm cut off by a sword, then one leg, then the other arm and then the other leg, yet keeps fighting. But Jack's ears were still way sharper than mine.

Bob silently crossed his fingers on both hands.

On Friday, February 14th, as I stepped out of the house with the dogs for their early-morning outing, the faint buzz of the phone reached my damaged ears. I hadn't left the hearing aids in overnight, so missed an emergency call earlier. Jack's oxygen level had fallen precipitously during the wee hours, down to 22 percent. They intubated him, put him on a ventilator and transferred him to intensive care.

"I'm not sure that's what he wanted," I told them. Here it was. The DNR problem.

I thought back to the conference Jack and I had with Wit. *No DNR. No DNI. No modification on the record for a situation where he was already hospitalized.* I dashed up to the ICU and found him on a ventilator. He would have a breathing test on Saturday. If that worked, they would try to remove it. Wit was already in Columbus by this time. But Charlotte couldn't get a flight until Sunday afternoon. The docs agreed to wait until she arrived.

That Sunday night, we were a crowd, Davises taking up half the ICU waiting room. In addition to Josh, Lorraine, Wit and I, Jack's sister, niece and nephew were present. Vincent was with Mémère, as he called his French grandmother. Only two at a time were allowed in to be with the patient, unconscious and breathing quietly. Charlotte breezed in from the airport, her hair swept back, stylish in snug leather joggers and a red cashmere turtleneck. We notified the medical team that we were all present.

"You can have four people in with him," one said. This was a big concession because it was a big moment. If Jack couldn't breathe without the ventilator, what happened next? We hadn't discussed it. I was aware of my own breath and tried to pace it.

My three children and I entered and looked at the DP, variously short for dear parent or dad person, as Josh had been calling the patient. We held our breaths, at least I held mine, as a doctor eased him off the ventilator. Jack breathed in and breathed out, like a rising tide. It was smooth. A wave of relief swept over me.

Afterwards Wit and Charlotte scrounged up dinner from Northstar Café, an arty hotspot close by with excellent vegetarian fare, and we made a mess of the waiting room with sloppy veggie burgers.

I had already met once with Dr. Norton from palliative care, with Wit joining from Phoenix on the phone. Dr. Norton's matter-of-fact questions and thoughts were soothing. We scheduled a family meeting with the palliative-care team for Monday morning, before Wit and Charlotte headed west and east.

In Jack's new room at the Brain and Spine Hospital, Wit talked us through what we were doing before the palliative-care team arrived. Palliative care was yet another term, one that Wit hadn't gone into when she first briefed Jack and me through DNRs, DNIs and living wills. Jack was semi-awake and tilted up slightly in the bed, tube still in his nose, plus various attachments. I never counted them. I was too exhausted and distracted.

"You can have pall-care at any time in a difficult illness, like MS," she explained to the four of us. "The goals are to optimize quality of life and cope with the illness. It's not hospice. It's not end-of-life care."

"So we're supposed to get a plan for that," one of us said.

At precisely 10 a.m. there was a rap on the door. The attending physician, a third-year resident, various med students and nurses poured into the room. Plus, I think, a respiratory technician followed. The pall-care doctor arrived with an assistant. Then came the parking-lot attendants, kitchen staff and the janitors. Maybe not the last three, though I had become friends with Maurice, who mopped the floor. The medical staff rotated like a windmill, so Maurice was the only member of the staff who was a constant in the month-long hospitalization.

Jack was wide awake and looked like he was paying attention.

Dr. Norton, the warm, friendly Indian pall-care doc whom I'd spoken to previously, introduced herself and asked, "Who will be speaking for the family?"

"I will," I said.

The doctor laid out the issues on the agenda and turned to me for a response.

Conscious of being observed, I was tongue-tied. This was a spectacle and I was on stage. *Where were my lines?* Wit, just behind me, moved a step forward in case she had to cover. I found my voice and said more or less the right things, namely that we needed help deciding where to go from here. I found myself leaning in towards my husband tilted up in his hospital bed, looking for comfort as much as comforting him.

After close to a week of glazed-eyed befuddlement, the patient was suddenly rational and wasn't about to surrender. Dr. Norton questioned him gently. "You've been through a lot and are stable now. We need to know what you're thinking and what you want done for you. How do you feel about your health?"

"Healthwise, I'm in a place where there are complications."

She asked him his wishes.

"I want to live to see my grandson grow up," Jack said as clearly as if he were at a conference table for an important meeting.

She verified what he was saying with a couple of other carefully phrased cues. "Okay, I understand, but you can't keep being fed through the nose," she said. "It doesn't provide enough continuous nourishment. And it gets extremely uncomfortable. If you can't eat yourself, you can have a feeding tube. Would you like to have a feeding tube put in?"

"Yes," Jack said.

"That will stay in *permanently*. Do you understand?"

"Yes. I want a feeding tube."

"And what about if you can't breathe. We can perform a tracheotomy if that happens and deliver air through a hole in your neck. Would you want us to do that?"

"Yes." Loud and clear, sealing the deal and blowing his family's minds.

I could have killed him. Okay, that wasn't what I was thinking. It's the first thing I wrote as I tried to remember that moment. "I could kill him" is what murder suspects, several of them, say offhandedly in a police procedural. I wanted it over, and, yes, that meant I wanted him dead. I was horrified and saddened that Jack didn't know what was happening to him and angry that he was reneging on the sensible strategy we'd proposed for both of us. I'd envisioned dying as a straightforward process. This was a torturous, unending, labyrinthine maze. The DP had just decided that he was willing to live life without fresh air, without food or wine, and unable to tell the difference between Fox News and PBS.

On the surface, for a fraught discussion, the palliative-care convention was handled as calmly, rationally and effectively as could be.

The American way of dying for old people is extremely expensive, but also extremely respectful of the individual's will to live. I appreciated that. Why did the meeting feel like an intrusive farce?

Dr. Norton stayed to talk for a minute. She put her finger on Jack's reaction. "This is what he's done every step of the way. It's one more adaptation."

After she left, the family quietly talked among ourselves.

"Wouldn't you know that he'd all of a sudden become perfectly lucid," Wit said, marveling. She summed up for us, saying the meeting was about a line in the sand, and the line had shifted. "We need to keep an eye out for cues that the line has shifted again. If mentioning Vincent doesn't produce a spark, it may be time to reassess. That and Steve's jokes."

Josh was angry and upset at the tone of the meeting and the arena-sized crowd. "What he needs is relentless optimism," he said, misty-eyed and visibly moved. "This other talk is worthless. Emphasize the positive... the feeding tube that will keep him going."

I felt for Josh. What were all those people doing in the room butting in on one of the most intimate possible discussions, infringing on this saddest of moments in a person's lifetime? I guessed some were there to learn. Why on us? Why not have just the attending physician and the palliative-care specialist, the only ones really needed. Jack had been violated, as if a surgeon had cut him open, despite what was supposed to be an atmosphere of caring. Me, too. Nonetheless, I had to take in that, although I felt like he was suffering, whatever was left of him did not. Amazingly, he wasn't in pain. I would do the best I could to support him, then as always.

The path was clear. I settled into my list of things to do. Jack would have the 'peg tube', as Wit called it, surgically installed. We would get him out of the hospital and into a rehab facility. And I was tasked with contacting hospice care for an 'informational session'. That 'hospice' word was out of the bag. I headed out to buy some extra-soft foods, since they would once again try him on those. I figured Brie and paté might tempt him.

It was 17 days from Jack's decision to fight on before the feeding mechanism was successfully installed, 17 days when the world was going mad and I lacked the mental capacity to take that in. Personally, I was in shock, the special shock of a soldier on a darkling plain, huddled in a muddy trench until ordered to attack, running and ducking towards the enemy, retreating again to the trenches and never pausing because if I paused I would spin out of control. Entropy would atomize me, then atomize the atoms.

Septuagenarian Bernie Sanders mopped up in the Nevada primary February 22nd. My thoughtful, dependable neighbors took Russell and Ari out when I could not. By the last week in February, walking the Poms around the pond in the early light, I noticed the hint of spring in the air, fresh green buds and blooms and daffodils showing their sunny yellow faces, which was as depressing as it was bracing. I remembered when winter was winter.

As Jack and I watched CNN on February 28th, if he was indeed paying attention, Governor Mike DeWine faced the cameras with a serious look and said Ohioans must have a sense of urgency about the novel Covid virus. That day, the Standard & Poor had its biggest drop since the 2008 global recession.

The first American died from the new variant of coronavirus in February 2020. News shows introduced SARS-CoV-2 or Covid-19, as a huge, heraldic image of a gray, round mass decorated with red, rounded spikes. Even Jack could pick out the image from his hospital bed, though I couldn't tell whether he understood what the fuss was about. The image became as familiar as the stars and stripes. The tiny reality, 100 nanometers in diameter, was a spiky crown surrounded by a membrane. The virus entered a human cell through the nose, mouth or eyes, attached itself to cells in the airway, pricked them open and sent in a bit of its own RNA. The duped human cell then made proteins to keep the body's immune system at bay and assembled new copies of the virus to pass on. Each infected cell could release millions of copies. Each infected human being could infect many more. There was no vaccine, no cure. The mortality rate seemed relatively low, but the virus spread so easily that the number of deaths could quickly add up.

Events were starting to be cancelled. I talked to my aunt, Mary, who said there was supposed to be a big do for the Council on World Affairs, but the gathering had to be aborted. The director asked if he could still pay her a visit, given that she was in a 'targeted' group. Her 91st birthday was coming up, and we'd already started to pick up on the risks to older folks. She laughed at how delicately he put it. They decided he could come to her house, but they would sit far apart and not shake hands.

Super Tuesday arrived, and Joe Biden unexpectedly cleaned up and was back in the race big time. The next day, March 4th, the Arnold, an annual event vital to the Columbus ego, was cancelled. Thousands of body builders and bikini-clad models from close to 100 countries could not descend on the city for the Arnold Schwarzenegger Sports Festival. Not a single case of Covid-19 had been identified in Ohio, and the governor took flack for being too cautious. Too bad he was right.

"I'm sort of fed up," Jack told me one endless evening.

You're fed up. Geez. So am I. Trying to channel Josh's wish to stay positive, I heard myself saying, "You're going to get the peg tube in and go to a good rehab place to get better. It will be quieter. Fewer people will be running in and out."

When you focus on being optimistic, you become optimistic. I found a room at the Westminster-Thurber rehabilitation 'studios'. Studios, indeed, as if they were comfy little apartments. The room was, in fact, appealing. It was small and simple rather like the Holiday Inn, though the bed looked flimsy even for a motel, much less a fragile patient newly released from the hospital. A window looked out on the busy parking lot and to the west you could see open sky. Steve or I or another helper could sit comfortably at the small, round table. I imagined being by Jack's side, reading or doing puzzles on my iPad or watching the TV on the wall directly across from the bed. I took in the relative silence of the place. I would keep fresh flowers on the table and make sure to bring suitable clothes from home, so he could look less like a patient. I could visit friends at the nearby independent-living, old-folks home after spending the mornings with Jack. Finally, a safe haven. He would get better, at least back to functioning as well as only a couple of months before. Maybe eventually we would go to the club and order soft-shell crabs. Planning is hoping.

An interventional radiologist, the specialist who could place the feeding tube, wheeled Jack downstairs for the operation. He couldn't find a good passageway. They sent Jack back upstairs. A gastroenterologist failed to insert the tube. A general surgeon was called in, since the operation was more complicated than originally expected. The weekend intervened and several days after that, more than two agonizing weeks after Jack firmly stated he wanted it, a peg tube was finally installed.

The respite lasted not weeks, not days, but hours. No caregiver was in the hospital room that night when Jack's nose began to spew out blood. I'd insisted that Steve take two nights off. The medical staff called in ear-nose-and-throat residents, not EMTs but ENTs, who fixed it. Wit said afterwards that it was extremely unusual for them even to be allowed in. The ENTs thought he had been fiddling with the nasal cannula.

The warning could not have been more in our face. People can complain of pain, aches, misery. They can have a fever or trouble breathing. Nothing says emergency more, however, than hemorrhage. Nonetheless, Jack was transferred to rehabilitation as scheduled on Saturday. I was intent on reaching the nirvana of rehab. The hospital was intent on following Medicare rules, satisfying the insurance company and freeing up a bed. I eagerly awaited my husband in the spic-and-span room at Westminster-Thurber. I'd brought a suitcase and stowed his T-shirts and supplies into the bureau drawers, even some shorts in case we could get them on him. I placed a vase of sunny yellow tulips on the table. The ambulance transport arrived with my beloved, so much more a patient than a husband, and I greeted him with crazed hope. The usual, hard-muscled strongmen transferred him to the bed, less adequate than ours at home, not to mention than at Brain and Spine. I tried to get Jack to take some food by mouth. If we could wean him off the feeding tube, we would be getting somewhere. The rehab studios had a pleasant, restful-looking dining room. I thought longingly that maybe in a few days we could wheel him in there. He didn't take the gelatin, soup or apple juice I offered, though. I saw a couple of patients in the hallway getting around with wheelchairs and envied them.

That night, blood began once again to explode from Jack's excavated nose. Steve was there. He and the rehab staff used towel after towel to soak up the flow and attempt to staunch the bleeding. Steve called me, distressed, complaining, "They don't have the right equipment."

If the hospital was starting to seem like home, so was the emergency room. Jack lay for hours on a bed in the hallway next to the nurses' station, along with several other patients. The bed had wheels, but there was nowhere to roll him. He wasn't conscious.

"His ENT is Dr. Bradley Otto," I told the medical staff in charge, once again stabbed with guilt for forgetting that he couldn't have anything up the nose.

Early the next morning, I arrived in the seemingly vast pre-op area, bed upon bed aligned against the wall, separated by flimsy, faintly patterned curtains. At the foot of Jack's bed a man was standing quietly in white surgical garb, a white skullcap on his head, looking at Jack. The scene was as still as a diorama of a medieval saint. As stiff and still and holy as a painting by Giotto. I could almost see a halo. I had been expecting a resident. It was Dr. Otto himself, there to personally to cauterize the septum. I would never my whole life forget my feeling of thankfulness at seeing competent, personable Dr. Otto, ready to step in even though I was quite sure it wasn't his day for surgery. I realized he must have authorized the ENT residents to staunch the bleeding the night before we insanely went through with the transfer to Westminster-Thurber.

That day, March 10th, as the virus spread across the world, our orange leader announced on national television: "Just stay calm. It'll go way." It didn't feel reassuring.

I waited in the atrium until about 7:30 p.m. for the post-operative briefing, intermittently consuming snack food from the machines, the old routine that Charlotte and I had perfected at Presby in Pittsburgh. I couldn't risk foraging anyplace else since I had no idea when Dr. Otto would arrive to brief me. Finally, he was there, still in his scrubs. Speaking quickly, he told me the feeding tube had been attached by magnets behind the septum. But Jack's septum was brittle from the prior surgery. The tube, meant to make things better, had cut right through the septum, causing the repetitive bleeding. Dr. Otto didn't talk down to me, for which I was grateful. The surgery had gone well, an intervention that could have been avoided if I'd remembered his nose was like a bottomless cup, with nothing between liquid and the soft, soft tissue of his brain.

Jack was admitted to Rhodes Hall, less pleasant than the Brain and Spine Hospital. He was separated from a roommate by a curtain. No more luxury of a private room. The cauterization took. OSU was at the point of asking every visitor if they had a fever and had been in touch with anybody diagnosed with the coronavirus. They still allowed more than one visitor at a time. It was mid-March. The WHO declared the virus a pandemic, and the disease began to tear across America like a tornado. Hospital visitors were restricted.

What do you do these days with someone who any thinking person would conclude is on his way out but has no 'do not resuscitate' order? The OSU docs said Jack's vitals were fine. Once again, they had no medical reason to keep him in the hospital. Fading away is not an emergency. The medical wizards cleared Jack for discharge, but we needed a new 'pre-certification' from the insurance company, which took days. Why do insurance companies get to break people's hearts? Luckily, I'd paid to hold the room at Westminster-Thurber and was desperate to get him back there and on track.

Jack was conscious, and for a whole day seemed to know what was going on. That was a Friday, and I stayed most of the day, as late as I could, trying to comfort him. Steve was to relieve me at 8:30 p.m. that evening. The patient seemed so with it that I thought I might as well go on home a little earlier, longing for my Poms and a good murder mystery.

Jack watched as I retrieved my coat and stood up. "I need my jacket," he said suddenly and seemed peeved that I wasn't moving faster. He thought he was in his wheelchair waiting for me to get him ready to go somewhere in the van.

"Where are we now?" I asked.

"The mall." This was one of three possible answers when a nurse routinely tested him on spatial orientation. The others were home and the hospital.

I pushed him, curious. "And where are we going?"

"Miranova." We'd talked for years about moving sometime to a riverside condo development downtown. Our unit would be on one floor and handy to much of the city. Instead, we installed an elevator in our two-story house in Blacklick.

I shed my jacket and waited for Steve.

The next day Jack was bundled in extra blankets and trundled down to Westminster-Thurber. Because of the pandemic, the rehab clinic had clamped down on visitors. Neither Steve nor I were allowed in. Once again, Jack lasted a whole night.

Wit was in town for the third time since Jack's hospitalization. She greeted him in his rehab room.

"Hey, Wit, can you get me out of my jacket and snow boots?" he said. She assured him that he was wearing neither. He repeated the request over and over and over until she left.

The next morning rehab stopped taking any visitors. Not Wit. Not me. Not Steve. Wit pleaded over the phone with Westminster-Thurber and the state ombudsman for an exception for Steve. No exceptions. All the staff I had met with at the rehab house seemed competent and dedicated to their jobs, but we knew by experience that a true emergency might be beyond their capabilities. How long would it take an ambulance to get there and the EMTs up the stairs or elevator? Too long? If I'd been wearing my professional hat, I would have understood we were talking about public-health policy. No exceptions. They lead to more exceptions. But I wasn't a member of the public. My family and I were desperate individuals. We needed a street-corner bureaucrat, meaning a cop or other official who gets away with judging a situation and adjusting just a little because it's the ethical thing to do. Once again, I thought of the economics professor long ago who disapproved of government funding for kidney transplants until he needed one himself.

It was Wit who took the 2 a.m. call Sunday morning. No problem with the nose; irregular breathing this time. Swiftly back to the

ER. A room in Rhodes Hall finally opened up sometime Sunday, March 15 th. They suctioned the lungs and tried to figure out what was going on.

The hospital was down to allowing one visitor at a time. Wit stayed while I went home for a nap. Jack was restless and in pain for the first time since the hospital ordeal began. "I hurt," he said, like a pleading child, and then cried out for help, for me and for his sister Donna, who we saw perhaps once a year, over and over and over.

"I hurt," he said again in a full, heartbreaking voice.

Our doctor daughter was overcome with her inability to help her father. She usually can go from patient to patient, solving a problem and moving on. Here she could do nothing except press to get pain meds ordered. She came home badly shaken and at the time told me only that her dad was in pain.

I drove up to the hospital and waited for the medication. Jack looked fragile and diminished but was still very much alive and agitated.

"I hurt," he howled in a voice I'd never heard.

I asked exactly what hurt. First Jack said his forehead, then his hand, then his lips. Everything.

"I give up," my husband said despairingly. "I give up... I give up. Vivian, I can't do this anymore." This sounded like the line in the sand shifting. I should have asked what he meant. Given a minute or so I might have explored his statement.

"Never give up," a nurse interrupted cheerfully.

A wave of fury boiled up from my gullet. I wanted to throttle her. Instead, what I said was, "At least not while you're waiting for oxycodone." Didn't she know that sometimes you *have* to give up?

My whole body was constricted in fear, sorrow and shared pain. I remembered to try breathing slowly, but it was ragged anyway. They got a dose of oxycodone into Jack and he relaxed. I did, too, a little.

On Monday, March 16th, Wit and I, she back home and joining by phone, had another conversation with a palliative-care doctor. A different one. You'd think they could have assigned us one doctor to share with and build trust. The trade-off here, Wit told me later, is that doctors don't have to work 120 hours a week these days, and that's about what it would take if they were continually available to particular patients. Nonetheless, after close to a month, the only person I had really gotten to know in the hospital was still Maurice, the janitor. The doctor asked us to consider our philosophy of care and what the DP would want. I pointed out that three people were not in the room.

Tuesday, the day of an all-family get-together with palliative care, was supposed to be primary day in Ohio, but that had been cancelled because of the coronavirus. The hospital was down to allowing one visitor per patient at a time, but they gave Josh an end-of-life exception. The medical powers had finally accepted the truth. The three girls, Wit, Charlotte and Lorraine, called in on cell phones. We held the meeting in a conference room, not Jack's shared hospital room. He was not in on the conversation this time. Two medical docs, yet another different pall-care doc, a social worker, a pall-care assistant and, I think, one other person, maybe a med student. It was a reasonable discussion. I was sick of reasonable discussions, keeping my head, trying to make a decision about another human being's death. The burden had shifted, I realized. It was more up to me than him.

Apparently the misery was still endurable as long as he had adequate pain medication. The docs did not consider the dose of oxycodone high. Jack was used to fighting every step down, and that's what he had been doing. But the hospital wanted him out. And I wanted it over. Wit pointed out that we weren't dealing with the same patient who attempted rehab only two weeks before. My husband had nothing left. He couldn't eat. They weren't even trying to give him anything by mouth. He had started to refuse blood draws because they hurt. He didn't know where he was. He knew me, thank goodness. Rehab wasn't an option if they wouldn't allow a caretaker.

As we talked, I looked out at a wall of innumerable other hospital windows. I wondered what other personally extraordinary decisions were being made in a time when every detail of life was extraordinary because of the spreading virus. I was exhausted and sick of the palliative-care people with their well-meaning, well-executed guidance. They were wonderfully thoughtful and communicative, and I resented them all. It was an intimate, demanding meeting and I was on the edge of collapse, willing myself to follow the thread of the conversation and make the best decision.

Hospice care, which Jack had shot down during a lucid moment weeks earlier, finally shot up to the top of the agenda. I lit up at the mention of a hospice that I knew was a place of comfort and calm. Russell, my gentle Pom, ministered there once, when a work colleague was in the last stages of a repeated cancer. A golf match was on the TV overhead to distract my friend. Russell lay on the bed with him and both of them fell asleep, my sweet, tender Pom on his back cuddled against him while his wife and I talked.

The pall-care doctor said we could try inpatient hospice for a few days and then see if Jack should be sent home. I didn't know a trial stay was an option. This was too good to be true. And it wasn't. Instead, we would end up bringing Jack back to the house he loved—a different Jack and a sad kind of being home.

A meeting with a hospice representative was scheduled for two days after the palliative-care assembly, two more interminably long days. Early that morning, a nurse phoned to say there was a problem. She had mentioned hospice care and Jack bridled. He didn't want it. I scurried up to Rhodes Hall, slowed down at the entrance by new procedures. They took my temperature, gave me a mask and asked questions that would become familiar: Had I been exposed to anyone with Covid? Had I felt sick? Had I traveled anywhere? I chafed at the interrogation, intent on getting upstairs to meet the intake nurse from the hospice. I found her waiting in the hospital corridor, a compact, business-like woman. From her crossed arms and frosty demeanor, it was immediately obvious that she had made up her mind. She said decisively Jack wasn't sick enough nor in a great deal of pain. "He could last for months and that's not what hospice is about," she added with an irritating little laugh.

She was judging by the feeding tube. She didn't like his being DNR-A at the hospital either. That one I'd never heard of, and nobody had told me it was his classification, DNR except for a cardiac arrest. Weren't they supposed to ask me? She thought we were using hospice for an inappropriate patient, one who wasn't close to death. She told me many people don't understand what hospice is about.

I didn't know what hospice was about? I unfortunately knew quite a bit.

The nurse said the alternative of a few days of inpatient care for evaluation was not one they offered. I'd been sold a bill of goods by the palliative-care team. The underlying issue, of course, was that the hospice was refusing many new inpatients because of the coronavirus. Good policy. That I could understand and accept. In addition, and a clincher, I knew visitors would be extremely limited.

In the last week, the only sign of life from Jack was when he was asked who the president was and he gave a sad little grin, a shadow of his old, enchanting smile. But in the time of the corona, he wasn't sick enough for hospice care.

The doctor on duty, Dr. Gordon; the hospice nurse; the social worker; the palliative-care assistant and I entered Jack's semi-private room. Whoever was on the other side of the curtain could hear everything. Dr. Gordon told Jack he was well enough to be discharged and asked whether he would like to go home to be in familiar surroundings and be comfortable. He did not say that a hospice service would manage his care. He did not tell Jack it was over.

Jack smiled wanly and said, "That would be wonderful."

At home that night, dogs walked, house locked up, and lying on my half of the bed, in swarmed the howler monkeys, maniacally jumped-up.

Nobody said anything about a DNR being in place. They didn't talk to me. The doctor cheated. Jack said no hospice. That's so simple. Hospice means dying. He's still fighting. I'm cheating. I'm cheating on him. A couple of weeks ago he was ready for ribs to be broken, throat cut open or whatever it took. I'm making another mistake. Like the nose. What am I supposed to do? Send him to the hospital again? He can't really want that. It would be crazy. It would be inhumane. Torture. Waterboarding.

The next morning—as I had throughout a month of blood, confusion, advice, helpful people who stuck around for an hour or two, crashes, semi-improvements, missed cues, bizarrely meaningful meetings, moments that seemed to be the end, malign outside forces moving closer and closer—I consulted my children, emailing them my worries in prose suitable for daytime. They had to be feeling terrible themselves but had consistently put on brave faces and helped to sort out the constantly changing struggle.

Wit emailed back: *Unless Dad can say where he is, know the month, year and have some idea of the day or date, he does not have the capacity to make his own decisions. I haven't seen him fully able to comprehend things for months, except for those amazing periods of lucidity when the subject is life and death. We can still ask him to make a decision, but not 'if your heart stopped, do you want us to try to restart it.' Almost everyone says 'yes' to that. If we ask, it should be more 'would you like us to do everything we can to keep you comfortable and out of pain? Or do you want medicines to try to help you stay alive even if it hurts?'*

With visitors prohibited even in nursing homes, many people were dying alone. I was lying to Jack but, if he could think about it at all, he would know going home was an improvement. Managing hospice care would be intense work and constant uncertainty punctuated by crises. At least it would be our comfortable, familiar surroundings. I would handle it.

On my way back home, I stopped at La Chatelaine, the French bakery and bistro, in Upper Arlington. Restaurants were going to need help, so in the spirit of supporting good causes, not to mention a desire to treat myself, I bought a bright-red cherry tart. The chef sat at a table disconsolate in his toque and white jacket.

In an even greater spirit of communal generosity, plus the fact that I wouldn't be able to eat an entire 11-inch tart, I cut away half for myself and, leaving the remainder in its pan, walked it over to my neighbor Carole.

Carole received the gift graciously, with a look of surprise beyond a thank-you. Had I committed a faux pas? If you make a stew or quiche, say, and have double the amount you can eat and you know your neighbors have a special need, illness, say, it's okay to take them half in its own container. It's not okay to take them leftovers. But if you're in a lifeboat together, the right thing is to share supplies. Given the times, I was trying to be neighborly.

On Saturday, March 21st, Jack finally came home looking like a ghost. His ashen face was gauntly thinner, cheeks sunken. Dark half-moon hollows shadowed his beautiful blue eyes. Up to a point, losing weight wouldn't have been a bad thing. A hollow stomach on my husband was unnatural. He looked like an incomplete full-body transplant. "Welcome home," I greeted him on the windy deck as two muscular men hauled his stretcher up the steps by the firewood. We certainly had made good use of such fellows over the last couple of years. It was the day the first Ohio Covid patient died and the day before Ohio State's president declared a university state of emergency.

"I'm glad to be home," he said in a stronger voice than in many days.

I made sure the hospital bed was placed so Jack would face the TV set at about where he used to park his wheelchair. I had made up the bed in homey patterned sheets and a red flannel pillowcase. Steve came. Wit had warned the transition might be rocky, but the DP seemed to settle in immediately. Ari wanted to be up on the bed and was calm and sweet when we let him try it. Russell at first ignored him. Then he seemed confused, moving his head from side to side the way he did when the choice was a treat if he obeyed 'come' or pursuit of a squirrel shaking its tail nearby. It was when the feeding tube was inserted that Russell freaked. He shivered uncontrollably at the intervention to Jack's body. What was the dog going through? Had he decided that Jack was not coming back, started to adjust, and now was utterly confused? Did he sense just how desperately ill Jack was and was dying? When Russell visited patients as a four-legged angel, most of the time he sat on their beds being petted and wondering when he would get a treat. Now he was so anxious I thought about feeding him peanut butter with a dose of the Valium prescribed for his terror of thunderstorms.

A nurse showed up soon after to bombard me with instructions. I wrote as fast as I could but couldn't take it all in. There was a whole notebook of handouts, however. A bunch of new meds arrived and others, such as the antidepressants, were cancelled. It didn't occur to me until later to wonder why Jack was still being given antidepressants and whether that contributed to his insane optimism and sheer desperation for survival.

I settled into a new phase of unknown duration, thinking about the hospice nurse's suggestion that Jack could live for months. A new aide, exceedingly gentle, took on the day shift on Sunday. She was an assistant respiratory therapist, ordinarily working at a nursing home. Now she was 'unnecessary staff' because of the virus. She had me cut his T-shirts down the back so they would be easier to get on and off. As I clipped, I thought about what that meant. He would never again be sat up to wear them. I hoped the aide would not involve me too much. I wanted to be cocooned in my perch above the family room imitating normalcy for those weeks or months the nurse said Jack could survive.

On Monday, Governor DeWine ratcheted up restrictions. The latest was self-isolation beginning at midnight Sunday night. Every Ohio adult would be reduced to texting, emailing, face-timing and phoning from their homes. Ohio children would be subjected to social isolation that might affect them their whole lives.

Josh and Lorraine came by. Around the same time, Charlotte and Wit both called in.

"They tell me you're buying a house," Jack said to Wit over the phone. She'd brought that up conversationally during his hospital stay. He'd never seemed to hear her. It was the last moment of lucidity.

I went to bed that evening, March 23rd, at about 10 p.m., leaving Steve with Jack. The DP had slept calmly most of the day. He was settled in for the next phase of life. Rachael was to relieve Steve while I slept. I heard nothing. At a little past 1:30 in the morning, Rachael woke me. Jack had been in pain for several hours. Steve had not gone home. The pair of them dealt with the crisis and had already called the hospice nurse who was on the way.

Jack's face was pale with a waxy sheen and he was having trouble breathing. I stood downstairs at the foot of his hospital bed listening to each wheezy, tortured breath, thinking they should have called me down earlier.

"You didn't tell me," I said to Rachael and Steve.

Arriving an hour later, the hospice nurse, a young woman with long black hair and an air of composure, took a gander. "I think he's actively dying," she said, and gave him 15mg oxycodone, 0.125 hyoscyamine, and settled on the remaining love seat with her laptop.

I looked at her, bewildered. "What are you doing?"

"I'm waiting for my supervisor to come."

"What about extra pain meds?"

"I've given him the dose he's on." She could repeat that up to a couple of times within a brief period.

"Don't hold back," I said, eyes watering, in pain at his agony. "It's what he wants." On this, I was dead certain. He wouldn't want to be in pain, even if it would kill him. The absence of pain until a couple of weeks ago had been remarkable and a major reason he could go on.

He was suffering; I was powerless. I called Josh, who rocketed over in a speedy 20 minutes. We didn't discuss what he did to the speed limit.

Another nurse came and gave him more end-of-life meds. She sent Josh off to pick up morphine. Kroger, the food-and-drugstore chain, didn't have any and he had to head to an all-night pharmacy farther away. This was the only time I wished Jack were an inpatient. The morphine would have arrived instantly. The hours crawled by as his chest continued to rise and fall.

"This is the worst part," said one nurse, a tall, lean and mellow middle-aged guy who showed up as dawn came. "He will be calmer again." He gave the dying about a day.

In the early afternoon, Donnie came over, bringing Lisal's homemade soup. We ate at the kitchen table. Josh stayed standing at the other end of the kitchen, closer to Steve and Jack. Jack's breathing was loud and ragged. I talked to Donnie, trying to be a good hostess. There was plenty of time to say our goodbyes, another day according to the nurse.

Steve was near Jack. "He's not breathing!" he called out to Donnie and me chatting in the kitchen and sipping soup.

Steve used his stethoscope and shook his head. Josh drew in his breath to stop the tears, shaking from head to foot. I walked towards the family room. Donnie followed and noticed a new painting over the fireplace mantel. He and Lisal had one by the same artist that inspired me to make the purchase at Christmas. I launched into an explanation of the painting. Neither of us had taken a good look at

Jack. Wit called. Steve had texted her the minute her dad died. She talked to Donnie briefly. As he passed the phone to me, Donnie gave me a goodbye kiss on the cheek and went home.

Wit sobbed that she hadn't been present for the end and I told her, "Look, nobody should feel any guilt. Everybody was terrific. I wasn't by his side when he died, and I have to forgive myself." That was a task yet to complete. It also happened to be Wit's 42nd birthday. I was sorry her birthday would forever be conflated with her father's death.

Shortly after, the male nurse appeared and in a quiet voice asked, "Mrs. Davis, what funeral home do you use?"

At first, stunned that my husband was dead only a few feet away in our family room, I couldn't comprehend what I was being asked. The floor seemed to shift under my feet. In slow motion, I floated into the kitchen, found the number for the closest Schoedinger, and silently handed it to him. When I returned to Jack's bedside, I saw Steve had covered his open mouth with a sheet. I pulled the sheet down. After a few minutes, Steve pulled up the sheet again. I placed my hand on his lifeless shoulder, already cooler. The second law of thermodynamics was kicking in. I knew all this, yet I couldn't grasp that my husband was *dead*. Again, in some magical mindwarp, I didn't know how he could breathe. Again, I pulled down the sheet.

A tsunami of guilt rushed in. I had failed my husband. I was eating in another room as he lay dying. The nurse had said it would be a day or so. How could I believe that? When he died, I wasn't holding his hand, maybe singing old Broadway show tunes. Actually, he would have hated the singing. I could have talked to him about our fantastic trips, how we'd seen the world together, how we'd raised a family, how we met, how we somehow stayed together when times were bad.

Josh left to rest after Lorraine showed up. Vincent was at Mémère's.

A knock on the back door. Black-suited men from Schoedinger trod in slowly with polite deference. Unlike the emergency squad, they had no need to hurry. They zipped up my husband's body in a bag. I didn't look, but at the harsh sound of the industrial-strength zipper, sobs rolled through my body. *What are they doing? Now there is no way in heaven or hell that he'll be able to breathe.*

My eyes overflowed with tears. I'd been pushed off a cliff, and gravity wasn't pulling me down.

Lorraine looked at me, her wide, intelligent hazel eyes brimming with compassion, and gave me a long, generous hug as the men from the funeral home hauled my beloved away through the sliding glass doors to the deck, the doors he had just entered four days before. Lorraine offered to stay or leave, or leave and come back later. Steeling myself and wiping away the tears, I told her it was fine to leave. That evening I filled out the death certificate online. The house was quiet. This was what I had been wanting. Or had I?

17

MOURNING IN THE TIME OF CORONA

Days after Jack's passing, my neighbor Carole texted to say she had a cough, a fever and a skull-busting headache. It was the virus, her doctor told her, but since her breathing was fine, she didn't need a test unless that changed. The words 'fever' and 'cough' were sickening. Leaning back in my ergonomic desk chair, I studied the text glaring from my phone and played back my visit to Carole's house: how I turned the doorknob to open the door with a naked right hand; how I walked in and stroked the smooth puppy fur of their adorable dachshund, Auggie; how I handed the cherry tart to Carole; how we spat at each other with chatter for several minutes; and how I turned the hazardous doorknob once again to leave.

Oh, no! I texted back, thinking *Uh oh. The plague is next door.* A frisson of fear crept up my gullet like a hairball.

Remaining calm, I called my internist, who'd been with me and Jack through multiple crises. Stay away from people for five days, she advised. She thought that was long enough for symptoms to appear. The advice online and on the news was two weeks. The medical community in truth knew little about the virus. It was as new to them as to everyone else. Carole's fever subsided. I texted Josh's family and Steve Buck to say I'd been exposed. Steve had a new job but still was coming around for cookies and to check on me. I 'self-quarantined' almost completely for two weeks, waiting for the slightest sign of sneezles or wheezles. Would the first sneezle come after the wheezle or before?

Carole recovered by the end of March. I hadn't caught anything but the heebie-jeebies.

I'd wanted the house empty, and it certainly was. Not only Jack himself, but the bustle of care had evaporated. Rachael and the others had moved on with new patients. During the night, unbidden, my hand crept over the gap between my side of the bed and Jack's. My fingers touched nothing but cold bedding. Russell slept against Jack's pillow. He lay on his back, paws splayed out and as relaxed as a yellow dust bunny. I wanted to tell Jack his dog missed him.

That spring, the whole blue planet was empty. The Place de la Concorde was empty, Grand Central Station was empty. Times Square, dark and deserted, looked like a scene from a disaster movie. New York City was a ghost town except for the heaving hospitals and morgues. Andrea Bocelli sang *Amazing Grace* at the Duomo cathedral in Milan, alone on the plaza, a tiny blind man with a huge voice in an immense space. Wild boars, mountain goats, peacocks and pelicans and other critters roamed deserted city streets, enjoying the freedom and calm of a quieter world. Surreal images danced on the TV screens showing medics floating around ambulances in special helmets and hazmat suits, and body bags being forklifted into fleets of freezer trucks.

Hyacinths had already bloomed and were fading. A hint of unshed tears continually gathered behind my eyelids, threatening to escape. I was able to stop them before that happened. If I yielded to sorrow, I didn't think I could control it. I thought I wanted stillness after Jack's death, but not the stillness of being locked up in my house while outside a dystopian nightmare raged.

Charlotte was confined to a tiny apartment in Brooklyn, working remotely from her advertising job with Saatchi & Saatchi in Manhattan. At first that didn't seem too bad, considering the elimination of commuting time. So for her 35th birthday in April,

I sent Charlotte a puppy of her own, William Blake, from Char's Pomeranians in Michigan. She would have entertainment and someone to stroke and cuddle up with. But I couldn't fly in to meet my 12-week-old grand-dog and had to settle for photos on Instagram, @ thepompoet.

Wit's world would soon be the opposite of empty. At first the Covid cases trickled into her emergency room in Arizona. She could see what was coming and railed against the shortages of protective gear for medical workers. Her masks were inadequate and Covid patients demand in-the-face care.

In probably the best policy decision of his entire term as president, Trump threw federal money at the development of vaccines. Bizarrely, he then refused to take charge or accept any responsibility for what he constantly referred to as the 'Chinese virus'. His followers jumped on board, the pandemic was a hoax. Struggling for every intake of breath for days before succumbing to a preventable death was a civil right written into the Constitution by God himself.

A full-out effort to test every man, woman and child would have made sense. But states and localities were on their own. Trump didn't like testing because it meant you found more cases. More cases looked bad, as if he weren't controlling the pandemic. It was surely a Democratic plot to bollux up his re-election plans. Like the Viking King Canute, vainly ordering the tide to ebb, Trump thought a force of nature driven by physics and biology should be under his demesne. The world was his fiefdom. Maybe he was onto something. His philosophy would be good for all kinds of things. Cancer, say. If you didn't test for it, there would be a lot less of it.

Most Ohioans continued to trust their governor and state health director on the appropriate response to Covid-19. At the national level, renowned immunologist Dr. Anthony Fauci patiently and repeatedly explained what we knew and didn't know about the raging disease. He was a voice of sanity amid the smokescreen of irresponsible ranting by the ignoramus in the White House.

The virus wasn't going away anytime soon. Where it raged, it was rational to be careful, but how? There were simple barricades. The coronavirus cell's oily membrane dissolved in soap: Wash your hands. It loved people at close quarters: Stay away from others. An infected person can anoint others with droplets merely by speaking: Wear a mask.

Who were you comfortable being near? Under what circumstances? How far away? With or without face covering? Who were your friends and family going to be willing to see (at a distance)? With what strictures? How would they communicate that? How would you know or sense it? Emily Post and Miss Manners have answers to everything from how to handle the creepy drunk cousin at Thanksgiving to how to eat corn on the cob delicately. How did you avoid being a virus vulgarian?

For those of us not at one extreme or another, 'social distance', used as a verb, was the new slogan and the new social skill. But how do people be social, their normal state, at a distance? To be sociable is to be close. In a climate of uncertainty and constantly shifting government restrictions, we had to make decisions on how much risk to take.

Social bubbles, small groups who could camp out together while we waited for vaccines, were an answer for those willing to take even a modicum of risk. For me, the thought of being entirely alone, day after day, was crushing. Death by grandchild seemed preferable, though that didn't come to a test. Thankfully, Josh and Lorraine decided to include me and Lorraine's mother in their bubble. At six, Vincent was a warm, moist bundle of hugs. Any germs on either of us were bound to be shared enthusiastically. First grade had been moved from the classroom, possibly the virus' dream home, to remote learning, so in the spring and into summer he saw almost no one outside the tight familial circle. For the parents, both busy IT consultants, working at home with even one super-lively child was a challenge. They could use my help.

Lorraine fought back the dark, hacking cloud of viral infection by turning the dining room into a mask factory. She developed a technique for creating pleated masks with elastic ear-straps, using vibrant, conversation-inducing patterns and colors. I told her she could make a few bucks on Etsy. They weren't for sale, but given out freely.

When I arrived one day, Vincent dashed in from the kitchen and hugged me hard. His head was up to my chin.

"In a couple of years, you'll break a rib if you do that, Vincenzo," I teased him.

He eyed my rib cage and looked worried.

"It's okay. I love your hugs," I reassured him. Grabbing my hand, he took me to see his new pet slug, Slimy, in a terrarium in the room that doubled as Lorraine's office and Vincent's home school. Later they set Vincent up elsewhere, using the rolltop desk that was once Josh's. Nothing was moving in the terrarium, though it was well landscaped with plants, dirt and rocks. I wondered silently if Slimy had turned turtle.

"Look at all these masks," I said as we went back to the living room. Lorraine had hung about 30 on a clothesline inside in front of the picture window. Vincent's friend Isaac and his family came by. Son, father, daughter and very pregnant mother stood in a row outside to choose from among the freshly made masks.

Vincent slapped his hand against the window. Isaac matched it finger for finger. Vincent moved his hand. Isaac slapped against it on other side of the glass, then moved farther. They were playing tag, the plague version.

"That was sad," I said to Vincent when they left. "The way you and Isaac followed each other's hands along the window when you couldn't play for real."

"It wasn't sad." He looked up at me with the serious explanatory expression he'd recently perfected. It was a lot like his father's. "We were having fun." Separation from friends had become routine for a peripatetic six-year-old to the point that he accepted it as normal.

I said muffled goodbyes with a cheery face covering tightly secured over my nose and mouth. The mask combined a white background and a bright French motif—the Eiffel Tower, a chicly groomed poodle and ice-cream cones.

Indoors, I kept to a routine I saw later was protective armor. In the evenings, when Jack and I had for so long taken comfort together, I nested on the love seat in the family room until precisely 5:30 in the afternoon, then watched a recorded episode of *Jeopardy!*, the game show. This was depressing in its own way, since the host, Alex Trebek, an American television icon, was dying of pancreatic cancer. Around six, I switched to a recording of the PBS *NewsHour* to rail against the antics of the dictator wannabe, my fury magnified by my inability to batter Jack with my run-on commentary. "Would you like me to shut up?" I'd have asked. "Yes," he would have said firmly. I smiled at the thought of his patience.

For years we had looked forward to Friday night when Mark Shields and David Brooks talked politics on the *NewsHour*. That spring, when all the reporters appeared remotely rather than in studios, sometimes with their pets or kids interrupting and stealing the show, Judy Woodruff, the anchor, asked them how things were going at home. Mark said he was happy with his wonderful companion of 50 years. Woodruff responded, "We all know Ann Shields." It was their 50th anniversary. Back in 1970, when Jack and I worked on the governor's campaign, Mark was our boss and Ann was office manager. More than that, they lived at Char and Dick's house, as I did at the time, while they looked for an apartment. The evenings they were with us, they enjoyed the three-course dinners served by uniformed domestic staff in the dining room papered with hand-painted Chinese wallpaper. "In Ireland a three-course meal is a six-pack and a boiled potato," laughed Mark one night. We knew he was funny and smart and it seemed a perfect career move when he became a quick-witted commentator.

As I sat there between the Poms, Ann came onto the PBS screen looking much the same as decades before. And Jack was not settled in his wheelchair as he should have been to meet my eyes with a knowing grin. The bastard.

I served myself dinner at 7 p.m. on the dot, eating salad greens with my fingers out of their plastic container and cooking up a stir-fry or heating up the third day of a beans-and-lentil dish at the stove while I listened to the news through my hearing aids. Several nights a week I treated myself to restaurant meals by curbside pickup or delivery. San Pellegrino was the drink of choice, or precisely measured glasses of wine. You're not supposed to drink alone, but surely that can't mean for months on end. After the NBC news, I switched to soothing, repetitive pap. I hardly watched the closed captioning, which meant I wasn't hearing much. Instead I devoted my rigidly scheduled minutes to crosswords, cryptograms or jigsaws. Over and over I clicked the remote to see how much time was left in the show, then glanced at the clock. Time slowly crept closer to 9 o'clock, when I could permit myself to go upstairs. Russell and Ari, warm and needy, were the only interruptions to a timetable worthy of a railroad.

It was a state of high anxiety clouded by miasmic boredom. As darkness settled behind the wide family-room sliding glass doors, thoughts of vandals crept in. I did not set the house alarm until bed-time because I might forget it was on when the dogs asked to be let out. An alarm fob, however, was close at hand to summon the secu-rity company. The door to the deck was firmly locked. I bought a pole that could be laid between doors to prevent sliding the movable section in case of a break-in. Cameras and motion-detecting lights were further deterrents.

You'd think that was plenty, given I could recall only one breach of our territory in close to 30 years of living in Windrush, and that was by an especially audacious raccoon. On a winter night a few years before this story, I put out premium bird seed with sunflowers and shelled peanuts on a metal pizza platter. I set the platter on a low wooden stool in the middle of the deck so the seeds wouldn't get soggy in the snow. It wasn't yet dark, so the motion-detecting lights weren't primed. In the gloaming, Scooby and Russell gave voice. I flipped a light switch. A fat raccoon sat on his haunches at the platter like a restaurant guest, his hands neatly popping sunflower seeds into his mouth. He looked me in the eye through his spectacles and called for a glass of Chianti. Service was slow, so he clanged on the edge of the platter, causing it to fall and spill, then departed without leaving a tip.

Those seemingly endless evenings shortly after Jack died, I would let the dogs out one more time, scared down to my toes that a gang of human predators would leap out of the bayberry bushes. Then, at exactly 9 p.m., I would head upstairs to my lonely bedroom with choc-olate or jelly beans and a glass of water. I read in bed, checking the clock every few minutes, and turned off the light at precisely 9:45 p.m.

During the day, the post-death to-do list kept me more gainfully occu-pied and other thoughts at bay: cremation, obituary, condolence letters and getting rid of the medical crap and Jack's clothes. Before the ritual burning, however, there was the matter of Jack's brain. He had wanted it donated to the Cleveland Clinic for research on MS. Because of Covid, the famed clinic wasn't taking brains. It was overwhelmed with the barely living. Josh checked with Ohio State. No brains, with or without cribriform plates. No cadavers. Josh and Lorraine called around: "Anyone want a complete human brain riddled with MS lesions?" Nobody could use a skeleton, carcass or offal of any kind. The OSU Brain and Spine Hospital, our home-away-from-home, was the answer. Jack's former business partner, Patti, knew the development officer. The neurology department had a new chair, Dr. Benjamin Segal, also director of the neuroscience research institute. His specialty was progressive MS, the kind Jack had and for which no significant treatment had been developed. Dr. Segal was working on a technique to regenerate nerve cells damaged by Jack's disease. We set up a fund within days and went ahead with the cremation.

When Schoedinger called to say that we could pick up my husband's charred remains, I slipped on a demure black-and-white dress suitable for a funeral, made sure every hair was in place and piled on the make-up. Josh drove us to the appointment. You can't just drop in. Understandably, they only take one family at a time. As we drove, I had a Monty Python sort of vision of families lining up at the funeral home door to receive their boxes, while other families filed out sadly holding them. Or it would be like the cartoon of the ATM machine where a line on one side waits for their money to spit out and a line on the other waits to steal it.

The Schoedinger rep had tried to upsell me on the container, but I insisted on the cheapest one. In the dimly-lit, well-appointed lobby, they handed over the heavy box in a purple bag with a gold ribbon. My family always thought funerals were a rip-off. I still have most of Dick's ashes in a plain Schoedinger brown box on my bookcase. They do pets as well as humans, and for many years, my father's ashes stood next to an identical box containing the remains of Hobbes, our golden retriever who could carry three tennis balls in his mouth at the same time. Jack and I finally paid a gardener to dig a hole for Hobbes. Donnie and Lisal had helped me scatter some of Dick's ashes in an illegal but suitable spot a few years before, but most remained parked on a shelf abutting my college class reunion books.

Because of the pandemic, it was impossible to schedule the party Jack had said he wanted instead of a memorial service back when his mind was working. Nor could we have a small family gathering to fulfill his wish of scattering the ashes in his beloved Windrush Pond. Covid had the world in cryogenic storage. My daughters thought an obituary in a printed newspaper was an ancient concept, and posted tributes on Facebook. Josh helped me write something that caught Jack's spirit as well as his accomplishments, to run in the Sunday edition of the *Columbus Dispatch*. He wrote the best line: "He was a fighter who finally had to accept the knockout blow, though not without, as he might say, taking the SOB all the way to the mat."

Condolence notes, thoughtful emails, phone calls and donations poured in, balm to my soul. Ingrid, whom I served with on the board of the Women's Fund of Central Ohio, wrote, *It's said that comfort slides in beside grief and gives us the strength to endure. I pray this for you.* I printed her email and pinned it on my bulletin board with the old *New Yorker* cartoons.

Two members of my writing group gave me a coffee-table book called *What It's Like To Be A Bird*. When I thanked them for David Sibley's tome that elucidates bird behavior from bobolinks to dabbling ducks, they reminded me that once I'd commented to the group that Jack always thought a more expensive present was a better one. I'd told them I was happy with a cheap little something to do with birds, like robin earrings, or whatever.

Hope is the thing with feathers, Emily Dickinson said. Riffling through the book, I wondered what would it be like to grow feathers. Uncomfortable, surely. Pinpricks all over the body. Scaly feet. Arms that started to pin together. Having to turn my head sideways to see.

When Char died in 2003 and Dick was already too sick to take on a task of answering condolence notes, not to mention too terrible a writer, Mary had taught me and my siblings to answer all notes individually, sitting the four of us down and splitting up the piles of notes and letters by who knew the correspondent best. "Now wasn't that easy," she'd said when we were more or less done.

When I wasn't crafting condolence notes carefully tailored to each correspondent, I tackled all Jack's stuff, starting with the medical supplies. Anything that might be foisted off on the Kidney Foundation, our chosen charity for used items, went into trash bags tied up tight. I posted a notice on Craigslist for a free electric wheelchair and, sadly, got some 60 responses. Steve ended up taking the much-used chariot to a needy neighbor of his.

Sifting through everything, where the spirit of our life together occupied every room, shelf and drawer, was daunting. Our closet was a sidle-in, not a walk-in, and too small for two people with reams of clothes. Closets in other bedrooms and Jack's office stored much of our wardrobe. I ordered new nonslip hangers and rearranged my clothes while I tossed Jack's into boxes. I decided to keep five of his nicest long-sleeved dress shirts and ended up with 14 neatly hung. There was so much of him in those natty shirts.

The basement yielded a banged-up metal strongbox that looked like it had been hauled over dirt roads in a 19th-century stagecoach. It was empty and ready for photos and other memorabilia. Jack's mother had left a slim manila envelope with childhood photos of 'Jackie' as she called him. One showed Jack at about the age of five rowing a full-sized boat on Buckeye Lake, a man-made lake east of Columbus where his parents had a summer home. There he was on a bench in the bow, firmly holding enormous oars in the water with tiny hands and heading out into the long lake. That was my guy. Always ready to row his own boat, even on the high seas.

Jack's office bookcase was a hodgepodge of work trophies, porcelain figures and books. I started with the glass and acrylic objects inscribed with the names of big buildings. Jack's best years were spent with the John W. Galbreath Company, a Columbus firm. Galbreath also bred racehorses and owned the Pittsburgh Pirates baseball team. Jack's job was to help put together the capital for commercial real-estate development. I admired the high-rise glass phallus with the outline of the Bank One Center in Columbus chiseled '$180,000,000 commercial paper and medium-term note financing', whatever that meant. Other objects celebrated imposing skyscrapers in Fort Lauderdale, Denver, Cincinnati, Houston and West Palm Beach.

I added Jack's Royal Copenhagen figures of a golden retriever and an Airedale terrier to a gap in the two whittled-down shelves of books. On the top shelf, I centered a framed black-and-white photo of Jack, low but centered in his wheelchair at a political fundraiser in the early 2000s. If you donated enough money, a photo op was included. Behind him were the candidate for governor of Ohio (who did win), the mayor of Columbus, me and then-Senator Barack Obama, whose left hand was gently placed on my shoulder. Because of Jack's wheelchair, we were in the front of the line for photos at that fundraiser. I suggested to Obama that he should run for president. He replied that he had much too much to do in the Senate. That was his standard response at the time.

The books left in Jack's bookcase were mostly our travel collection and miscellaneous Aubrey-Maturin historical tales by Patrick O'Brian of the truly high seas. Glancing at the collection, France, Italy, Joshua Tree National Park, Botswana, Argentina, so many adventures, sent me reeling through time, flashing back on the many days and nights we spent together at those spectacular places. In Botswana and South Africa we were on safari. How on earth could Jack go on a safari? Because the game watching is all from an open Land Rover. You weren't allowed to walk, much less run. The big cats and other dangerous animals take in the vehicle as a strange multi-headed thing. It's when they see legs that you become tasty prey. I figured that out when Babette and I went to Tanzania a few years before. When we visited the Ngorongoro Crater, the world's largest volcanic caldera and, from the windy lookout point, I glanced down at the vastness of an area where possibly our most ancient ancestors roamed and had the peculiar feeling that Africa was home. I knew I could get Jack there.

In Botswana, warthogs rutted under our cabin and hippos used the passage between cabins to ramble loudly down to the Okavango River to wallow in paddies of water hyacinth. In South Africa, we eyed prides of lions lazing in the shade, giraffes munching on treetops, great herds of elephants and Cape buffalo on the acacia-studded grasslands. We saw a stunningly beautiful leopard halfway up a tree guarding his freshly killed antelope dinner, warily looking out for the carrion eaters next in line. Our guide spied a black rhino sniffing something in the far distance. The bull rhino took off at an amazing speed. The guide turned the Land Rover off-road and followed at a terrifying pace, rattling through bushes and over saplings until the rhino found what he was looking for, a female in estrus. Sitting as still as we could, we watched as the male approached to within a dozen feet of her. She kept grazing on the succulent green leaves and shoots from a bush-willow, never deigning to note her Romeo. He left, disconsolate.

We boarded cruise ships, though I can be seasick in a swimming pool. Cruises were ideal for old people with limited mobility and perfect snowbird retreats. I would have preferred something less structured and confining, but for us they were great ways to escape the erratic, gloomy and often bone-chilling Ohio winters. One of our triumphs was a shore excursion to Iguazu Falls while on a cruise to South America and the coast of Antarctica. Iguazu Falls is far inland on the border between Argentina and Brazil.

"Are we making a mistake?" Jack asked as we pulled ourselves together for a long day.

"Maybe," I said as I loaded my backpack with clothes for both cold and drenching spray. "But it's too late."

The first leg was a two-and-a-half-hour plane flight. As we landed, I could see plumes of spray from the falls in the far distance. Next was a bus to the national park. Through crowds of fellow tourists, we were herded onto an open train for the last leg. I unfolded the wheelchair one last time and the bus driver helped Jack stagger from the bus into the waiting chariot. The path to the falls, a long, two-way bridge made of bumpy, latticed metal, seemed to go on forever. The wheelchair's tires were like a racing bike, thin and light, and Jack slipped farther down in the chair at every bump. We had to stop frequently for me to put my hands under his shoulders and yank him back up, then, with effort, start up again.

"Poor Niagara," Eleanor Roosevelt said when she saw Iguazu Falls. She was right. It was worth it. It was spellbinding.

Standing above the roar of the water that drops off immense cliffs in a subtropical setting, we took in the many swift streams storming down to dark cauldrons. We were in misty air and musty scents. Aside from the throng of sweaty tourists, it was wilderness as vast and miraculous as it can be. Many hours later, as we hungrily downed hamburgers and Argentine wine in our shipboard room, I said, "You'd think we climbed Everest."

Jack laughed and glanced at me slyly. "For us, that was Everest."

After I finished clearing out and tidying the study, I stood back and admired the sparse, pared-down shelves. It was a shrine that would evoke good memories every time I went into the office, which would be often since it housed the printer.

"How do like your blue-eyed boy Mister Death?" I murmured the words by E.E. Cummings to myself.

Cremation, obituary, condolences and selected memorabilia. I'd taken care of it and left it all behind. I pulled out *1000 Places to See Before You Die* from the bookshelf. As soon as the epidemic subsided, I could travel, free from a disabled partner, to all the far-flung wild places still waiting. I could go to Morocco and see the medieval medinas and treasure-filled bazaars of Marrakech; and the Galápagos Islands to see the blue-footed boobies and giant tortoises. I don't believe in bucket lists, which are both too ambitious and too constraining. I hardly wanted to leave my own house, but could imagine a time of exciting new adventures to escape the gloom and sadness, to live again. In the meantime, competence and attention to detail were getting me through. I was doing it right. No way was I going to waste time weeping and sleeping.

I wasn't going to get off that easy. Denial is supposed to be a stage of grief, not a modus vivendi. The heart and brain work from different premises.

My friends and neighbors, especially the more vulnerable ones, had their hatches tightly battened down. They still had to eat, though. They solved that with the rapidly multiplying delivery services, ordered online and picked up their takeouts in parking lots in the safety of their cars. My two refrigerators and freezers had started out packed. Thoughtful folks brought soup to my door after Jack's death, though I didn't have guests to help eat it and had a freezer practically packed with soup. Even the milk was the long-lasting organic type. Toilet paper was the hottest commodity in the country, spawning endless amusing videos.

Tulips popped up in flamboyant pinks and purples, oranges and yellows that defied depression, until the deer came around and ate them. When the last half-gallon container of milk went light in April, I was forced to conjure up provisions, don a mask and brave the new world. I wanted to see what I was buying, but mostly I was curious enough to venture abroad, namely to the interior of Kroger, the local grocery. They reserved 7 to 8 a.m. for seniors like me to purchase their bags of Nature Valley Big & Crunchy Oats.

I set an alarm to vibrate on my phone and slept with the phone against my side. When it shook at 6 a.m., I let the dogs out the patio door to the deck for a minute for a leak and postponed coffee till after my adventure outside. This meant I was still half asleep and drifting drowsily. A greenish super moon hung huge and low, touching the western horizon directly in front of my car, like a coronavirus without the spikes. Super moons occur when the moon is closest to the earth, and this was one of two in 2020. I pointed moonward in the murky, pre-dawn darkness to hunt down rice and sugar, feeling like I could become E.T., my little BMW with all-wheel drive a silhouette framed by a luminous circle.

As I walked across the parking lot, shadows of masked customers as vague as dreams appeared against the dim store windows, lined up lamblike outside the entrance. I slipped my Parisian-themed mask over my ears, finding spots for the elastic along with the hearing-aid loops and eyeglass frames. The sidewalk was marked off in X's made of red tape placed six feet apart. In the darkness, I moved slowly from X to X behind the next shopper. No one spoke.

Immediately inside, 'essential' workers were spraying down the carts with sanitizer. Food-delivery employees, like healthcare workers, garbage collectors and meat packers, were among those required to work to keep the country going. They didn't get to choose their level of risk. I grabbed a cart's damp handle. I tried not to think of the grocery store scene in *Contagion*, which had gone viral on streaming sites as people searched for relevant, if often overimaginative, explanations for what was happening. In the movie, the protagonist father and his daughter visit a dark, looted store. The shelves are empty, the aisles abandoned. Except that around one corner, a pitiful woman, all skin, bones and pallor, suddenly appears, pleading for help. Father and daughter leg it out of the store.

From 28 years of shopping at that Gahanna Kroger, I knew the layout like a mouse that's run the same maze thousands of times. It would be fresh vegetables to shampoo to check-out in a dash. The thought of what Jack would like for dinner snuck in and had to be painfully rejected, then the more positive thought that I could buy all the broccoli and cauliflower I wanted. I concentrated on keeping my upper eyelids dropped halfway over my eyes to avoid a deer-in-the-headlights look. I'm prone to that, and it would go over even worse than usual with the mask covering my nose and mouth. The store was surreally dark. It seemed like half the lights high up on the warehouse-style rafters were on hold for the official opening time. I turned up the volume on my hearing aids to listen for coughs, and peered around the end of every aisle for zombies. The cotton mask sucked itself tight against my nostrils with each breath, hot and stifling.

The toilet paper wasn't in the usual place. Out of curiosity, I veered off course and found it in a far back corner, where stores stock the most popular items so the customers have to pass the beckoning cookies and waffles on their way. On the vast metal shelves, a few lonely rolls of toilet paper sat like pigeons on a telephone wire. ONE PER CUSTOMER read the sign, making me feel I must grab one. Scarcity breeds greed, and in normal times, higher prices. I refrained from greed. Breathing slowly to ward off panic, I approached the rice. On a shelf ordinarily packed tight with white, brown and wild mixtures, a lone bag of basmati rice lay on its back. A score. I spied sugar and hefted a five-pound bag into the cart. I planned to bake banana bread and maybe a chocolate dacquoise layered with meringue and crème fraîche. I ended up making the banana bread, adding the special touch of slivered almonds, just shy of their sell-by date.

Weeks were turning into months. By senior hour at the supermarket daylight had arrived. It was dawning on Americans that the virus wasn't going away anytime soon. Holing up like a crated puppy wasn't healthy, I knew, especially the lock-step dedication to the clock. In mid-April, I was burnt out by all the shutdowns and stay-at-home orders and, in the name of sanity, willing to cheat a little on my nuclear family bubble. As always, the dogs demanded exercise and I jolly well wasn't going to wear a mask while strolling my open suburban neighborhood. As always, I ran into neighbors. Like me they were maskless. We struck an unspoken bargain to skip the masks but attempt to honor the recommended six-foot distance. As always, the dogs needed to sniff each other, leashes got tangled and we limbo danced around and under to undo them, coming within inches of dangerous human noses and mouths. A couple invited me to join them on their daily three-mile walks, maskless, and often drifting closer than six feet. I would sneak closer to hear better. Clemie kept up an extremely brisk pace. After the first walk, I offered to peel off because we were going faster than my short, dachshund legs could trundle. They let me set the pace.

Bob, who'd visited Jack in the hospital and was surprised to find me with a preacher, snuck over to my house, along with his wife Nancy. Nancy—a child psychologist specializing in learning difficulties—was in the midst of editing a new edition of her book on how children learn math and arrived frazzled. Bob and Nancy thought they had already had mild cases of Covid, so they were safer than I, unvaccinated and destined to remain so until the next winter. They brought over a Passover meal and we devoured chopped liver, matzoh, beef bourguignon, potato latkes and a flourless chocolate cake. Bob and Nancy were our closest friends as a couple. Our normal outing was to a movie theatre and dinner. After our illicit Passover dinner, the three of us huddled around the TV and watched the movie *Emma*. It was a lawless evening. I felt like we were hiding from the Egyptians.

One evening I dabbed concealer over the age spots on my face, brushed on face powder, a smudge of sparkly blue eyeshadow and a dab of lipstick called pink truffle. I pulled on a bright red top and hooked on dangly silver earrings. My shorts were a loose-fitting yellow pair that over the years had grown suitable only for gardening. I was shoeless, hadn't shaved, and the black stubble on my legs looked like a burnt-out forest. I was ready to be sociable on Zoom.

As the pandemic swept across the world and everyone sheltered at home, Zoom was the savior app for meetings, get-togethers, virtual classes, virtual cocktails, coffee or quiz nights with friends. Click a couple of times and you joined a gathering of bodiless rectangles, up to 25 on a page. Over the spring and summer I attended Zoom meetings with my reading, writing and research clubs, political fund-raisers, lectures and even a shiva. I zoomed every Thursday afternoon with three close college friends. That worked so well that I contacted my three closest high-school friends, whom I had barely spoken to since we graduated in 1963. Noon eastern time was the feasible saddle point for meetings. One long-ago classmate joined in her pajamas from Vancouver Island, one from New Mexico, and one heading toward her bedtime in Athens.

Most of my friends are *d'un certain âge* and a few ran into trouble with the app. We hadn't used Skype, Zoom's precursor, much, if at all, so were way behind on video get-togethers. Early on I added a virtual background of the pond at sunset on Zoom. It didn't always work and, unfortunately, the default when it crashed was a photo of Scooby, my Pomeranian who died several years ago. He did look attentive, but it was embarrassing when he popped up on a briefing on Ohio prospects by the chair of the Democratic National Committee, a meeting to which I would ordinarily not be invited.

The Hungry Readers, my book group, was called that because we always met for dinner. This worked perfectly when we read a translation of Dante, or a book authored by a Japanese writer; not so well when the genre was science fiction or the topic famine or climate change. With restaurants closed, we were reduced to zooming. I hadn't quite finished *Americanah*, so zipped through the last pages in a few minutes and found myself a big glass of Pellegrino. I tilted my screen up a bit in case Ari demanded a lap.

Kirk, Joe, Bob, Brit, Indira and I joined the meeting at 7 p.m. sharp. Daniel was supposed to show up, but no Daniel rectangle appeared. So we dove in. Kirk, Bob and Joe objected to the sections on African hairdos, all the weaving and lengthening. Brit and I said we liked those scenes.

I phoned Daniel. "Click on the blue line," I instructed, and his full name showed up white on the black screen, then a moving human face.

"Why do you want to avoid long names?" Indira asked the others. "Indian names can be long, too–"

"You're on, Daniel," Kirk cut in, "But you have to unmute. Scroll to the bottom of the screen and a menu will show up."

"I can relate to Ifemelu," Indira continued. "Like when she talks about that American who says of every photo of a black woman 'she's beautiful'. People tell me my name is beautiful and my accent. I hate that."

"I can hear you now," Daniel yelled over her. The yellow ceiling took up most of his screen. And what you could see of him was jaundiced, too.

"Garble, garble," Joe said as if he was under water. He was visible down to his eyeglasses.

"We can't hear you, Joe." Kirk's shiny bald head aimed at the camera like a full moon.

Leaning into his screen to be better heard, Joe was garbling louder as though he was drowning in a swimming pool.

From my lap, Ari turned up his foxy head and chirped a request to come up on the desk. I moved the keyboard and put Ari in front of the screen. He slipped a bit, then lay down. *Why bother with etiquette on this crazy call?* The screen turned white. Zoom had cut us off. Knowing they gave you more time if you started over, I clicked back in. Go ahead and imagine how that worked.

As the days in hibernation dragged on, my still somewhat curly, white locks were growing wild, falling in a mop over my face. It was great that my hair had grown back so well after chemo, but I was turning into Andy Warhol. It may have been considered a high-risk venture, but I had to have a haircut. By the end of May, the virus spread rampantly like Californian wildfires, ravaging whole towns and cities and filling up morgues. U.S. Covid deaths passed 100,000, the most of any country in the world. In Ohio, we started to hear about a friend of a friend, or a friend, or a cousin who died.

Still, hair salons were open again. My stylist Vini called. Of course she needed the work. She assured me the salon was taking all precautions.

I opened the door to the beauty salon and became stout Balboa staring at the Pacific, or an English scholar opening Seamus Heaney's translation of Beowulf. I was in the same room as eight or nine three-dimensional human beings. It felt like a crowd at Ohio Stadium. I soaked up the startling way they turned, stood, sat and motioned with their arms and heads. Each styling station was separated by a thick but see-through plastic shower curtain. I took in the fruity, tangy, astringent smells of shampoos, sprays and nail polish remover.

Vini greeted me warmly through her mask and took my temperature. "97.1!" she crowed in the same tone of voice she'd used for the past 20 years to inform me how wonderfully thick my hair was. After a good dose of sanitizer to my hands, I followed her to be shampooed.

Back at Vini's station, I eyed the client next to me through the wavy plastic that made her look as if she were under water. She wore pink rain boots too wide at the calf that left a long gap of fat, flabby exposed leg before a dress began just below the hips. *Yuch!* A stylist across the way wore olive slacks and a matching mask. *Cute.* I examined the length of the woman's pants, trying to remember the name of the designer who said no woman should wear capris, or any pants that aren't full length. I was having a catty little feast. I reminded myself that we were in a strip mall in Ohio and everyone in the salon was past their prime. None of us was beautiful, not even the style-conscious gay guy who had finally owned up to his age. Once he was a fashion-forward fellow. No more ponytail or skin-tight, sexy pants now. His curly hair was short and gray. He wore old jeans and a T-shirt.

Facing a mirror, I spied another one on the other side of the parlor that reflected a hypnotizing view of the back of my head. I feasted my eyes on the shelves of hair products. When Vini's scissors arrived at the hair around my ears, she expertly lifted the elastic on my mask and evened up. She quickly snipped away and swept up a thick pile of white clippings.

I left feeling lighter and happier, but disappointed that the usual bowl of tiny Tootsie Roll Pops had disappeared from the cash-register counter. I always dug my hands through to try to find an orange one, or at least avoid root beer. Tootsie Roll Pops were no longer safe.

Across the street, kids caroused naked-faced in the playground. A line of uniformly masked adults patiently waited six feet apart from right to left to be admitted to the butcher shop. A truck selling soft ice cream was parked outside the shop, with a line of laughing teenagers at the social distance of a litter of kittens.

I crossed the street to my car, shaded by tall, mature maples. Those kids, laughing and touching, were born in this century. They had no memory of the Vietnam War, though the maples might have been saplings then. I wondered whether any of the old-growth trees were alive when the great influenza of 1918 arrived. The sycamores in Northam Park were likely to go back that far. Char's aunt Lottie, for whom she was named, died of the Spanish flu. Thus, my Charlotte was descended from a plague victim of 100 years ago. Like it or not, we were living in a historic moment.

With the warmer weather and easing of the lockdown, we would be allowed to play tennis. The word came down from the Greater Columbus Tennis Association. Team play would begin late and end early. There would be no playoffs, championships or banquets. No socializing after matches. Players must not stay and play for fun once their matches were completed. And edicts came down from the New Albany Country Club, where I had signed up for the 2019 platinum team. We no longer had the women-power to field a gold team. The club would not be providing water dispensers, benches, umbrellas or hand towels on the courts. Two bathrooms would be open and sanitized every two hours. No ball machines. No entering that enclosed hotbed of disease, the clubhouse. All playing members must adhere to the six-feet-apart rule at all times.

Both the GCTA and New Albany imposed strict rules on handling the tennis balls. Members were to provide their own. No using your hands to pass balls back and forth, only your racket. How was this going to work? No matter the precautions, it seemed a bigger risk than rolling through the grocery store, having my hair cut or even hugging my grandchild. I needed exercise, but was getting it through long walks. It was stupidity itself to go out on a tennis court. Tennis may not a contact sport, but it still requires contact. I signed up, longing for escape from my shrunken world that was even more constricted than it had to be.

My fellow players arrived at practice masked and, avoiding the table with the furled umbrella, established mounds of purses and water bottles six-feet apart along the low fence dividing the courts. We dropped the masks, unleashed the rackets from their cases and formed a wide circle around our new pros. I leaned in as close as possible to be able to hear.

The coaches split us up into two courts and warmed us up with mini-tennis, then began a drill with two players back on one side and two at the net on the other. The pro fed the balls from a hopper to the players who stayed at the base line. No lobs allowed on the first return. The idea was to get the ball past the net players between them or to either side. Play out the point. It was a good drill.

At the end of the round the baskets were empty. I started to pick up balls on my racket, only to be told off by the pro, "No! We have to pick them up."

Gathering the far-flung balls after a round of practice was usually the players' duty. It was hot and tedious but part of the deal. I was guiltily off the hook.

On Sunday, I stopped at the tennis shop to buy a couple of cans of balls for non-team recreational play. The salesgirl opened a can and used a permanent marker to put my member number on each ball. I gave her a look that said *seriously?* "I'll skip buying the second can," I told her. I didn't want it staying open for weeks while the balls lost their tightness.

Our recreational group gathered, a little closer than at practice, but still maintaining a distance from the table with its furled umbrella. There were eight of us, or two courts. That would mean we needed 16 balls. Without a word, we opened our usual two cans, three balls per court, and warmed up with mini-tennis. When a ball went errant we scooped it up and tamed it with the racket. One came my way on the fly and I caught it with my left hand.

"You touched it," my partner said, shocked. I would be sickening seven other women with my asymptomatic Covid. They would sicken hundreds more. Small children would die in Tanzania and Afghanistan.

The incriminating tennis ball in my hand, I pressed it against my tennis skirt as if both of us were about to be arrested. I shouldn't have bothered. As we played, it became obvious that it took way too much effort to avoid picking up a ball or passing one to your partner who was serving. The best we could do was avoid touching each other.

The sun went higher, and it was sizzling on the court. On side-changes, I took off my cap and mopped my forehead, face and neck with my towel brought from home. It was soaked by the end of the first set. So was my bra, and my artificial breasts felt like a couple of lead weights. There were no chairs, but one player flopped down on the ground to rest. Another had brought a fold-up chair and parked in a shady corner to catch her breath.

We looked at the umbrella. Again in silent agreement, one of us unfurled it while another secured it to the post. A deep primeval instinct called on us to be like cattle under a tree at midday, side by side and nose to nose. Politely, two or three at a time, we crept under the cool shadow of the umbrella maintaining two or three feet of distance.

The worst of the first wave of disease passed many areas of the country. Arizona was among the states where dim-witted residents ignored the danger. By summer, Wit's hospital was a ship of fools. They arrived struggling for oxygen. Wit intubated them, sticking a hard metal tube down the throat and deep into the windpipe, then hooked them up to a ventilator. By then she had enough protective equipment, masks, shields, boots and space suits. She was about my height and the outfit heavy and stifling. The preventive personal equipment was meant to be worn for a few minutes while visiting a single patient. She was stuck in it 12 hours a day, with two half-hour breaks for food.

As autumn loomed, I asked Josh and Lorraine if I could invite my friend Melodee to their backyard for lunch and a chat with Vincent and me. A retired scientist, Melodee was in determined isolation. She knew what 100-nanometer-size viruses can do. We had agreed early on that it was safe enough for the two of us to walk together along the swiftly running Scioto River, brisk rambles where we looked out for mallard and the striking merganser ducks with fan-shaped collapsible crests that made them look like punk rockers.

Vincent knew Melodee well and adored her. She had accompanied Lorraine and him on the neighborhood candy rounds at Halloween, Vincent sporting Lorraine's latest remarkable handmade costume, a vampire squid. The creature can turn itself inside out, and Lorraine created a burgundy cloak with eight 'legs' that Vincent could flip up to reveal strings of battery-powered lights on each limb demonstrating the creature's bioluminescence. The squid has unusually large eyes for its size, and the huge ones attached to Vincent's forehead were scarier than any store-bought costume.

The careful parents agreed Melodee could pay a call. I brought grain-and-corn salads for the adults and mac 'n' cheese for the child. I was heartily sick of curbside pickup. Many restaurants had opened up patios for outdoor eating at a distance. Neither Melodee nor I had tried that yet.

Vincent and I headed outside and down the driveway to greet Melodee. There she was, on foot, a slim woman in a rose-colored dress and sunhat, looking more like she was taking a stroll on the Riviera than Upper Arlington. Melodee's preferred means of transportation was the bicycle. She biked to her 50th college reunion at Bryn Mawr, over 500 miles away. Not only did she have a Ph.D. in biochemistry, but she served on the law review at the Ohio State law school and her apple pie had won a prize. Melodee was a renaissance woman with a two-wheeler.

We all went around the back of the house. I brought out the food. Vincent and I sat at the white patio table, our chairs almost touching. Melodee perched on a bench six full feet away. Vincent played with his tablet, which was updated that day with second-grade apps. School would start the next week virtually, with hopes that in-person class could begin a few weeks after that if Ohio's threat level from the virus went down a bit.

He found a brand-new translating app, and I helped him choose Spanish. "Hello, my name is Vincent."

"*Hola, me llamo* Vincent," said the tablet.

"Listen," he said excitedly to Melodee and rushed toward her. She warned him off.

I had a book to share, *Wilding*, which I adored. I put it on the table and backed away. From a distance, she figured out she had read the book and refused to walk over and touch it.

Vincent was poking the machine and getting it to make strange noises. He laughed as he approached Melodee again.

"No, no, no," she said to him.

"Let me look at that," I said, encouraging him to come to me instead.

He was translating from Dutch to Catalan. There are two problems with that. Nobody present spoke either language. And he was speaking English when the machine thought it was Dutch and did its best to make it so.

Melodee watched Vincent leaning against me from the edge of his chair, engrossed in his new acquisition. "I don't know when I'll see my children and grandchildren again," she said wistfully. Her grown children and her grandchildren were scattered from Vancouver Island to New York City.

Sammy the cat wandered onto the terrace and went straight for Melodee. He curled his slinky tiger-striped body around her legs from nose to long tail.

"They can carry the virus," she said, a story that was circulating. Much later we learned that cats and dogs can indeed carry the virus but didn't spread it to humans. I was horrified to learn over a year later that the first canine victim was a Pomeranian in China. Melodee loved cats, and it was hard for her to resist leaning down to pet this sweet ginger boy. Sammy knew a patsy when he saw one and jumped up on her chair, purring like a cheetah and swishing his stripy tail. She shrank away, then picked him up and put him carefully on the stone patio.

A few leaves had fallen and scattered near us. As the afternoon light faded, cicadas clicked their late-summer songs.

It was six months since the virus arrived. We had bargained with the plague to construct new, more circumspect social lives, each according to our understanding of the risks. The miasma of immediate fear had lifted. I had basic supplies and services. I had even risked it all on a tennis court. Who knew when it would be safe to go inside a restaurant, see a concert in person or board a plane for a long-overdue vacation?

We had to decide who we saw, if anybody, and how. We had to negotiate how we ate, how we dressed and how we worked, if one had work at all. It upended our errands. It upended our entertainment. First it seemed like a scary rumor. Then it arrived. Then it went on. New more virulent variants threatened. Then we wondered what normal would become.

I had taken care of grieving for my husband and could cross it off the list. All I needed was for the world to open up again.

A door was about to fling wide, letting in a windstorm.

The reckoning didn't arrive that summer of 2020, or even the fall. It was after my arm was jabbed with two doses of the new Pfizer vaccine the next winter, a full year after Jack's death, that grief felled me. The inoculations went smoothly, with my age group scheduled well before many. I was whisked through both times at the Ohio State University's basketball arena. I took a selfie with a statue of Brutus Buckeye, the team mascot, at the exit. A buckeye is a form of nut with dark and light brown coloration, supposedly resembling the eye of a deer and bringing good luck. Thus, Brutus' head is a large nut with a rictus of a smiley face. It's hard to believe he would strike fear into the heart of the enemy, like a Wolverine or a Spartan. That's left for the players. In the photograph, Brutus had a thumbs-up, and so did I.

The windstorm that had been brewing in my head and in my heart, when it crashed in out of the blue, battered me senseless. I had tried to force it to the bottom of the pond, and there it was whirling to the surface, a terrifying mass that could not be ignored. I'd had cancer and so far was okay. I'd lost my husband slowly and miserably. Covid was supposedly under control. I deserved to be happy, to embrace the future, which suddenly seemed to have evaporated. *What future? I might as well be dead like Jack.*

The reality of death had not penetrated. Like Joan Didion, who'd lost her husband and daughter in the space of two years, I had been a 'cool customer'. It's how I got through Jack's last illness. In the aftermath, I'd done my best to turn into an automaton. Mourning is self-indulgence. Our culture teaches us that we're supposed to enjoy ourselves and not impose our sadness on others. We're to meet and conquer the many practical consequences efficiently and quickly. I'd slept fine through most nights during the pandemic, except when aging Russell needed to be let out in the wee hours. Now I tossed and turned, annoying the dogs. I felt exposed and alone, more alone than while we were locked up against the pandemic. If this was my new life, who was I? Did I even care? It turns out that a cool customer is someone in a state of mind-numbed shock. When the anesthetic starts to wear off, she's in trouble.

A critical observer would say boredom had something to do with it. I'd been through my own illness, Jack's and the chaos of Covid, all keeping me busy in their morbid ways. The politics of 2020 and into 2021 required huge amounts of attention and worry. Joe Biden was president, finally, and, though it would soon be clear that America's problems were not going away, that ceaseless Red/Blue war was in a hiatus. I needed to get going, but had no energy. Isolation during the height of the first rounds of the pandemic had a purpose. Now I was shrinking into isolation for no discernible reason.

Skeptically, I opened *How to Go on Living When Someone You Love Dies* by Therese Rando. A clunky title. Grieving for dummies, probably. The point I picked up was that grief doesn't follow a pre-dictable schedule. It will be with you forever, not proceeding in stages as Kübler-Ross originally posited, and not necessarily steadily reced-ing but more likely hitting the bereaved in surprising waves. Further, and this took my breath away, she explained that if the true work of grieving is interrupted by 'circumstantial factors', the survivor won't make progress. Experts see a 'six-month phenomenon', a coming out of a daze after everyday life has recommenced. That was me, and it was the circumstance of Covid that froze my adjustment, if I was going to make one. I'd thought Jack's seemingly endless decline had amply prepared me for his final passing.

Joan Didion's husband, the writer John Gregory Dunne, died of a heart attack, instantly and unexpectedly, over dinner one evening. The literature says an anticipated death can be better prepared for, but to watch out for premature detachment. I got the picture. I wasn't hallucinating that Jack was suddenly going to appear and need a fresh T-shirt, but he was still with me in a visceral way.

Acknowledge the death, experience the pain, that's the expert advice. Putting mourning on the bookshelf with the boxes of ashes was so much more appealing on the surface, and what the literature recommended would consume time, a commodity we can't count on. It was infuriating that more work had to be put into this stupid grieving project when I could get sick again myself any time. But a continuing state of despair was worse.

As I thought about it, I realized that I was even more sensitive than some people to being cut off from a loved one. The primal wound that haunted my life was my birth mother's disappearance into mental illness far away, across the Atlantic Ocean. Ever after, that had a way of reasserting itself in morbid moods those around me couldn't understand.

Poor Wit, when she decided to attend McGill University in Montreal, one of the finest universities on the continent, got a taste of that abiding, devastating response to absence. Her choice hit me as if she was going to leave the country forever, though Montreal is only ten hours away from Columbus. I would never see her again. The symbol of McGill is a martlet, a mythical swallow-like bird without feet that can never land and is continuously in flight. Interpreted positively, that means that education and adventure never end. I saw a tiny, lonely creature unprotected by gravity. I paced the house through the nights. I pleaded with Wit to choose someplace else. Jack mediated the crazy situation, and, funny thing, she didn't disappear for all time simply by leaving for college.

Perhaps my life's worst episode of that type of fear and despair followed a miscarriage a few years after Wit was born and well before Charlotte. To determine the health of the fetus, the doctors performed an amniocentesis, an invasive prenatal test, at the second trimester, when things are supposed to be well along. The fetus was healthy. Jack and I were ecstatic. We had been trying for the third child for a long time. Within a week, I had lost that feeling of being relentlessly taken over by something glorious. The ob-gyn couldn't find a heartbeat. He sent me to the hospital for a sonogram.

As one nurse rolled the damp sensor over my large belly that had abruptly stopped swelling, she said to the other, "It's gone."

I heard her perfectly well but still asked, "What's going on?"

"That's for the doctor to say," she answered.

After the surgery to remove the dead baby—and abortion-rights advocate that I am, it was a baby in my mind—I held onto Jack all night for three days except when he was holding onto me. If we let go, I was sure I would fly into the night of outer space. I would have clung to Jack during the day, too, but behaved as normally as I could manage. Now, some three decades later, there was no one to hold onto.

I had already had to settle into a new body. With the loss of Jack I would have to settle into a new soul. I'd have to accept that he'd been my dearest friend, companion and lover, but not 'my other half'. Being married means having someone to be alone with and yet feel complete. You can think of it as the fingers of two hands being intertwined, suggested Therese Rando in her book *How to Keep on Living*. Your job is to unlace them. I remembered all those nights curled in each other's arms like double integral signs, those times where we were as close as if our ribs were intertwined. It went deeper and was more intimate than unlacing fingers. I would have to disentangle all those ribs.

I always dreaded the thought of becoming a widow. Someone who is left out of parties because she is alone, a shadow of her spouse. I knew too many widows, and I didn't want to be one. With friends I had to be sociable, self-aware and friendly. With Jack I was never 'on'. I was my silly, complicated self. I needed my best friend to bicker with over whether the dishwasher was full enough to start or to ask me whether I'd set the alarm system when of course I had. I needed someone whose sentences I could complete and who could complete mine, so that we both complained we'd been married too long.

First crone, now widow. Next it would be 'late'.

I thought about how in 2018, I motored to a fundraiser for Senator Sherrod Brown with Sen. Kamala Harris as the featured speaker. The venue would be hard to negotiate for Jack's wheelchair, so he stayed home with an aide. At a moment when I had the Ohio senator to myself, after the future vice president's pitch for Sherrod, he sat on the back of a sofa, long legs extended casually and arms crossed. The press always refers to Brown as rumpled, and his disheveled hair and barely articulated clothes attested to that description.

"Where's Jack?" he asked. "Usually you bring him."

It struck me as a funny thing to say. On the way home, I realized that I always thought that Jack and I attended events and parties, especially political ones, together, neither in the lead. For decades I had done the usual wifely things, but I knew Jack never had any doubt I was co-leader of the family. If somebody thought I'd been the power behind the wheelchair, it hadn't felt that way.

Now, trying to envision my future, I could see the Senator's point of view. I had become more and more a caregiver over the long decades of Jack's illness. My husband had become physically dependent and, then, horrifyingly, mentally dependent. It had changed the relationship. Gradually he became mostly patient rather than husband, and observers could see that. Viewed positively, I ought to be prepared to live on my own.

I decided to be more effective about mourning than in 2020. To leave Jack behind, I needed to escape our house, sell it, move on to something new without as many rooms, as much furniture and silverware handed down through generations. All that cookware when I was barely cooking. I had to get out of the family room. There was no family there. I'd made myself exquisitely safe, like zipping myself up in a body bag. Somebody told me that if I was nervous about intruders scaling the wooden deck to the backyard, I should buy curtains and let the dogs out of the front door. That wasn't the treatment for existential fear and loneliness.

I needed to get out of a house that held too many memories.

What they called 'independent living' might solve the problem. I wanted people around me, security, and a plan for my decline. Someplace like Westminster-Thurber, where we'd satisfied the insurance companies by twice checking Jack into rehabilitation when he was beyond rehabilitating. It had a full array of care, starting with quietly available background support in well-designed apartments with high ceilings and good views. A balance of freedom and security. Westminster-Thurber, smack in the buzzy heart of downtown, was about ten minutes from Josh's house on the freeway as well as the OSU hospital. I had friends there and their living quarters were pleasant, their cars downstairs in a garage. There were all kinds of outings, even rides to the grocery store. I inquired about pets. They would take two small dogs, I found out, though Russell and Ari would need to be interviewed first. I could pull away from the past life and create one.

Josh accompanied me on a tour with a tiny, slim guide. As I knew, the units were more than livable. Two bedrooms, one for my office. A many-windowed sunroom with plenty of light and places to perch and a balcony overlooking the rehabilitated houses of Victorian Village. A good-sized dining-living room combo for someone unlikely to host a big party. I would have to give away hundreds of books but there was room for a bookcase or two.

Doubt crept in as we descended to the first floor to see the community amenities. The empty dining room looked dreary and sad. Like a Holiday Inn, I remembered from the rehab debacle. The tiny shed of a library was overwhelmed by a machine as big as an oven for magnifying print. Along the long, low-lit corridor we passed residents and their walkers or scooters. They were ancient as sycamores, all of them. I was getting a bad feeling. This didn't seem different from a rest home, the euphemism my father and grandmother used for the rigid dependency my psycho birth mother was reduced to. It was a waiting room.

The three of us sat down to talk about nuts and bolts, meaning money and availability. I could afford it and units in a new building, which would be ready in two years, were selling fast.

After we left, I immediately asked Josh, "What do you think?"

"I think you seem to have your heart set on it," he said dispassionately and shrugged his shoulders.

"You don't like it?"

"I can't see you here. You don't need it."

"But I will. That's the idea."

There was no sign that Josh would feel relieved if I were more supervised. "I can help more with things in the house," he said. "And I can be at your place in 20 minutes."

Please don't go that fast. Thirty minutes, I hope, I thought to myself.

"Why don't you text me each morning?" he suggested helpfully. "If I don't hear from you by ten, I'll text to check."

Here was this business of giving over the reins to the children that first emerged when Jack was in the hospital in Pittsburgh in 2010, and I insisted on driving instead of Lorraine. With Jack gone, I was being asked to lean on Josh, to be one of those whiny, complaining weights on the younger generation. But so far he was willing to take it on, the local one, so the one with most responsibility. The relationship with my kids had indeed shifted, and I was grateful that they cared. I thought about how well we had worked together through their father's last illness. It wasn't so bad to ride in the passenger seat if you agreed on where you were going.

At home, I realized that the independent living that had seemed to beckon had hidden fences. The formal entryway to the new apartments, a full lobby with a staff person as greeter, would be on the interior side of the compound, looking out to the vast parking lot. It wasn't only that I couldn't simply let the pups out a door, front or back. The set-up was for the justifiable goal of protecting the residents. What I saw was that they were walled off from city life. It would be like being trapped forever on a cruise ship, a luxurious façade for containment. Shore excursions where you superficially took in the sights and bought souvenir penguin earrings. Sitting at the same table with the same people night after night, sharing organ recitals about our latest medical woes.

If Jack were there, maybe he'd make us move. I wasn't sure of that, but it had always been his initiative that found us a more suitable home than the last, me complaining all the way. There was the kitchen remodeling in 2001 that brought us our much-used and appreciated screen porch as well as expanded cooking and seating space. At the time, I swore I'd have 'Jack's fucking kitchen' cut into the granite countertop. But he was right.

After Josh dropped me off back home, settling in my usual perch in the family room, Ari chewing on a rawhide on the carpet and Russell out of sight, snoozing in the kitchen, I asked myself the essential question: *Would I suffer any less from bereavement?*

I imagined myself in one of those lovely apartments just as lonely and feeling no safer or happier. I could see the rungs on the ladder. You went down one step at a time, and court six was hospice. The descent could be disrupted by new disease, or accident any time, just like in Windrush. The sense of security would be as false as the rigid life I had been living.

There's no perfect place to live, but Windrush had to be close. A new family had moved in two doors down with three small children and another on the way. The neighborhood was growing younger. Carole and Blair, three doors down, sat on their front porch in the evenings sipping wine and would sometimes invite me to join them. How lucky can you be to live in a neighborhood where people rock or sit on a front porch and kids play street hockey? A short walk with Russell and Ari meant popping out the door. A longer walk with only Russell meant heading around the pond. For more than a half mile, I would head out alone, with old Russell sweetly begging to go along as I gently closed the door. I'd just had a bald cypress installed in the backyard, figuring it would do well with climate change. The little ginkgo planted a few years ago was flourishing. The shingled oak was a volunteer and not the most beautiful tree, keeping its brown leaves all winter long, but it wanted to be there with the others. Like all living things, trees are members of an interdependent community.

I'd lost Jack and I'd lost my life with him. The world had shut down and now was opening again, maybe. There was no choice but to live in it. I could start simply, by choosing appealing movies or shows, giving the dogs an extra after-dinner walk and seeking out people to get together with at mealtime. Instead of facing the TV, I would linger on the screen porch and read long into the warm summer evenings, with the fireflies lighting up the sky and crickets singing their nightly songs. Dinner could be whatever I wanted, wherever I wanted.

One morning at the break of dawn, waking up earlier than usual, I texted, *Hey, how about a walk?* to friends I missed, and as we rambled I listened to their troubles and tried to be helpful. The crazy world of American politics demanded attention, not to mention threats to individual freedom and communal welfare.

First things first, I would have the party Jack once envisioned as a memorial gathering. It would be at my house—mine, not ours anymore. I would put mosquito-repellent candles on the deck and pull out several bottles of Jack's collection of fine Bordeaux from the cellar for uncorking. With luck the cheerful gathering, more wake than funeral, would be outdoors and spill onto the grassy lawn sweeping down to the pond. At the end of the party, a little tipsy and fully sated with traditional family hors d'oeuvres like chicken livers and water chestnuts wrapped in bacon and oatmeal cookies from a recipe passed down for generations, a few of us would gather on the deep end of the pond. The kids and I would take turns scattering the ashes as beady-eyed Canada geese floated at a safe social distance. It wouldn't be windy, so the ashes wouldn't blow back in our faces, the way they did in *The Big Lebowski*. They would travel the surface ripples with the bass and blue gills, descendants of the ones Jack stocked the pond with many years ago. Slowly they would settle to the bottom with the enormous carp that control the algae. I would throw the depressing utilitarian metal box in the recycling bin. The grief would roll in again in crashing waves, but I would steel myself to observe them as a separate almost-whole person capable of forming new memories.

ACKNOWLEDGMENTS

How can I know who I am if I don't know who
I was? And how can I know who I was unless I
can read what I write? That's memoir.

Britt Collins, my brilliant editor, helped me unravel the last five crazy years. Britt is, in fact, a Brit, and our only real disagreement was when her spellcheck substituted 'Labour Day' for the American holiday. She encouraged me and stuck with me through many laborious drafts. She prodded me to tweak my "taut" style and add more "colour." I urge self-publishing writers to spring for an editor. Their tumblers can take your pitted rock and help it metamorphize into something like the smooth, shining gemstone you imagined. A book requires both art and its complement, craft. Britt is a pro at both.

Xavier Comas of CoverKitchen designed the book's cover, with Britt helping to make it catchy and present a clear message about the content. My artistic daughter Charlotte Mary Davis also lent a hand with the cover.

Several writer friends read *Down on Court Five* at various stages of gestation. Marty Ross-Dolen critiqued the very first version. I knew it needed work when her first question after reading it was,

"What is the book about?" Cathy Berkeley and George Kingson slogged through later, better versions. And Cathy once again went through the almost-final gemstone wannabe. Thanks to all for their clear eyes, red pencils and encouragement.

My informal Thurber Writing Group critiqued many nascent chapters and scenes. Thank you Shelley Hoben, Shirley Nyhan, Melanie Garrabrant, Janette McDonald and Rita Kearns. The group grew out of a course in creative nonfiction at Thurber House, taught by Katherine Matthews. We've been meeting for 13 years.

Special thanks go to my daughter Dr. Wit Koenig, now medical director of a hospital emergency department, for helping get the medical terms and procedures right. I am boundlessly grateful to every one of the medical staff who kept Jack and me going, and, like all of us, to medical workers worldwide who braved the uncertainties and ceaseless workload of waves of Covid.

My son, Joshua Witkind Davis, and daughter-in-law, Lorraine van Dommelen Davis, were all in whenever needed. I thank my whole family for being there in easy times and hard.

Thanks to Steve Buck, Rachael Ertel and all the other caregivers. Steve, the one with us the longest and steadiest, was unflagging in his devotion to Jack. All my friends were supportive, and there are way too many to thank. I want to single out Marty Ross-Dolen and Jody Altschule for donating their valuable time to shepherd me through cancer treatment.

Any remaining errors are, of course, my responsibility.

Made in the USA
Middletown, DE
25 April 2022

64630004R00123